Having a Martha Home the Mary Way

Having a Martha Home the Mary Way

31 DAYS TO A CLEAN HOUSE
AND A SATISFIED SOUL

- Sarah Mae -

TYNDALE®
MOMENTUM

An Imprint of Tyndale House Publishers, Inc.

Visit Tyndale online at www.tyndale.com.

Visit Tyndale Momentum online at www.tyndalemomentum.com.

Tyndale Momentum and the Tyndale Momentum logo are registered trademarks of Tyndale House Publishers, Inc. Tyndale Momentum is an imprint of Tyndale House Publishers, Inc., Carol Stream, Illinois 60188.

Having a Martha Home the Mary Way: 31 Days to a Clean House and a Satisfied Soul

Copyright © 2016 by Sarah Mae. All rights reserved.

Previously published as the e-book *31 Days to Clean*.

Cover and interior illustrations are the property of their respective copyright holders and all rights are reserved. Coffee mug © by MakeMediaCo/Creative Market; couch © Aleksandra Novakovic/Dollar Photo Club; coach and chair © by Handicraft/Creative Market; house icon © by Oodles Doodles/Creative Market; washer and vacuum © akedeka/Shutterstock; flowers © by Graphic Box/CreativeMarket; wreaths © by Webvilla/CreativeMarket; pleasantly Plump icons © Denise's Shop/CreativeMarket; Flatilicious icons © Pixel Bazaar/CreativeMarket; retro pattern © Vitek Prchal/CreativeMarket; restroom icon © lightenir/Dollar Photo Club; duster icon © skarin/Dollar Photo Club; sugar plums script © Sweet Type/CreativeMarket.

Author photograph copyright © 2015 by Kim Deloach. All rights reserved.

Designed by Jennifer Ghionzoli

Published in association with the literary agency of The Fedd Agency, doing business at PO Box 341973, Austin, TX, 78734.

Unless otherwise indicated, all Scripture quotations are taken from the New American Standard Bible,® copyright © 1960, 1962, 1963, 1968, 1971, 1972, 1973, 1975, 1977, 1995 by The Lockman Foundation. Used by permission.

Scripture quotations marked ESV are taken from *The Holy Bible*, English Standard Version® (ESV®), copyright © 2001 by Crossway, a publishing ministry of Good News Publishers. Used by permission. All rights reserved.

Scripture quotations marked NIV are taken from the Holy Bible, *New International Version*,® NIV.® Copyright © 1973, 1978, 1984, 2011 by Biblica, Inc.® Used by permission. All rights reserved worldwide.

Scripture quotations marked AMPC are taken from the *Amplified Bible, Classic Edition*,® copyright © 1954, 1958, 1962, 1964, 1965, 1987 by The Lockman Foundation. Used by permission.

Scripture quotations marked NLT are taken from the *Holy Bible*, New Living Translation, copyright © 1996, 2004, 2015 by Tyndale House Foundation. Used by permission of Tyndale House Publishers, Inc., Carol Stream, Illinois 60188. All rights reserved.

Scripture quotations marked MSG are taken from *THE MESSAGE* by Eugene H. Peterson, copyright © 1993, 1995, 1996, 2000, 2001, 2002. Used by permission of NavPress Publishing Group. All rights reserved.

Library of Congress Cataloging-in-Publication Data

Names: Mae, Sarah, date, author.

Title: Having a Martha home the Mary way : 31 days to a clean house and a satisfied soul / Sarah Mae.

Other titles: 31 days to clean

Description: Carol Stream, IL : Tyndale Momentum, 2016. | Rev. ed. of: 31 days to clean. | Includes bibliographical references.

Identifiers: LCCN 2015040601 | ISBN 9781414372624 (sc : alk. paper)

Subjects: LCSH: Home—Religious aspects--Christianity. | Christian women—Religious life. | Home economics—Miscellanea.

Classification: LCC BR115.H56 M34 2016 | DDC 248.8/43--dc23 LC record available at http://lccn.loc.gov/2015040601

Printed in the United States of America

22 21 20 19 18 17 16
7   6   5   4   3   2   1

This book is for everyone out there who needs to know that being a "good" homemaker has less to do with having a clean home and more to do with loving others well.

Table of Contents

Foreword

THIS BOOK IS HOW I met my best friend. She's the one who wrote it, but five years ago when she released pieces of it as a bit of a pamphlet e-book, I read it for no real reason other than I needed to do something. Cleaning my house was one of the somethings.

You've been there, right? My guess is you're there RIGHT NOW since you're holding these pages this very minute. Among the things bidding for my attention at that time in my own life was a request from our church to lead a women's Bible study group. I was in a bit of a dry season, which led me to a really deep conversation with myself that went something like this:

"I'm feeling uninspired right now, and my house is a wreck—a wreck, I tell you! But if I lead a study on cleaning, then I'll actually be forced to follow through with it. Those who lead are forced to do."

If there were a prize for superspiritual reasons for doing things, I would absolutely not have even made it through a preliminary round. But since they asked, and since a friend of mine told me about Sarah's project *31 Days to Clean*, I submitted the class proposal and ordered the book afterward. Uninspired people often don't do their homework.

When I actually downloaded the e-book, I realized that my best-laid plan needed to be adjusted something fierce. I didn't know that e-books are typically not nearly as long as standard printed books, and here I'd just signed up to lead a fourteen-week study. The title alone—*31 Days to Clean*—should have tipped me off that I would come up short on material if I'd actually bothered to do the math. But then again, pertinent things like timing and preplanning weren't exactly on my unmotivated radar.

I freaked out for a day and then figured that since I wasn't inspired, maybe if I asked the Lord, He'd give me a nugget to fill up the rest of the time.

And He did.

I used parts of Sarah Mae's e-book in conjunction with some of my own Bible study on the why behind the Mary and Martha challenges, and something incredible happened in that group.

Women were changed.

What began as a kick in the pants to do the laundry and wipe down the baseboards turned into a refocusing of a roomful of women who had all lost their way somewhere in the midst of the mundane. The instructions they were reading weren't just a call to action to ruthless purging in hopes of seeing the floor of their closets again—they were an invitation to explore the why and the how together.

I remember thinking to myself in the midst of that study, *If I ever wrote a book and it changed people, I'd sure want to know.*

So even though I didn't know her personally, I e-mailed Sarah Mae just to tell her . . . to encourage her . . . and to let her know that somewhere in the midst of cleaning closets and writing mission statements, a whole group of women unlocked passions for their homes and families and friends —parts of their lives that had collected some cobwebs over the years.

I never expected to hear back from her, but the Lord had plans for this woman and me, and He used this book to start them.

What began as a project to get her own heart in order has now turned into this full book. Over the past several years, Sarah has fine-tuned the projects, missions, and motivations within these pages. She has dug deeper in her soul, and the Lord has unlocked new content that I believe will move you into the experience I had with those women years ago. It's time to get going, girls—grab a friend, grab a hand, and grab a mop—we've got some tidying up to do. We may start clearing off counters and floors, but in the end, I think what we will find is rearranged hearts.

So as you turn these pages and explore the Mary inside of you (the one who lounges at the feet of guests and loves well) and the Martha (who is on the move and gets stuff done), I think you will find that the cobwebs you most enjoy removing are the ones in your soul.

Logan Wolfram
Author, Speaker, and Host of Allume Ministries

Gentle Homemaking

I USED TO THINK that if my home was clean, I was a good homemaker.

Over the years, as I've reflected on my life and have recalled memories of growing up, I've come to the conclusion that it is not a clean house that defines good homemaking, but rather a warm, inviting place that is filled with love.

As a matter of fact, I would prefer to get rid of the word *good* altogether and replace it with *gentle*. I want to cultivate the art of "gentle homemaking," which is the ability to be gentle and kind with ourselves in the process of making and keeping a home while being gentle and kind to those around us.

It's so easy to beat ourselves up as well as cast blame on those closest to us, isn't it? We are quick to condemn ourselves and our efforts when things don't work out the way we envisioned. And once we feel frustrated with ourselves, it's a natural progression to accuse those around us. Our husbands and children can so easily get the brunt of our own feelings of inadequacy. I have often accused myself of being a homemaking failure. But you know, the only thing those condemning voices do is paralyze us from getting on with our lives, trusting God in our weaknesses, and moving forward in faith.

When we can move forward without the condemnation of our sometimes meager efforts, we can become better, gentler homemakers and lovers of others.

Now as to the actual chaos and practical business of homemaking, I have found that loving others and creating peace happens when there is less mess.

When I can't walk from the bedroom door to my child's bed without stepping on something, there is chaos.

When I walk into the kitchen and it's too messy to make a nutritious meal (who wants to cook in a mess?), my family misses out on a good meal prepared by me.

When I get up in the morning and can't find something to wear because I didn't do laundry *again*, I feel out of sorts and cranky. Or I'm late for an appointment because I have to search high and low for something I can throw on to make me presentable.

The point is, when we have less chaos in the house (via a mess), we have less chaos in our souls, and when we have less chaos in our souls, we have more energy and capacity to love.

How Does a Clean(ish) Home Love Others Well?
Love can be (and usually is) very practical. When I make sure I have clothes for my kids to wear, I have loved them

practically. When I can get into the kitchen and cook good meals, I have loved my family practically. When I can extend a spur-of-the-moment invitation to a friend who needs to talk, and the surroundings are inviting, I have loved her practically.

Can we love our family and others who come into our home if everything is in a jumble? Of course! This book isn't a legalistic, do-exactly-as-I-say-or-else approach because I know firsthand that a messy home doesn't define who we are. I am simply offering possible ways to add more serenity and minimize the disarray in our homes. My goal with this book and with my life is not to worry about being a homemaker who rocks at cleaning, but rather resolve to be a homemaker who is kind and gentle and has a quiet soul and an available home. Maybe you want that as well?

Let's do that; let's journey together in learning how to quiet our souls, love well, and care for our homes practically.

Why Would a Woman Who Doesn't Like Cleaning Write a Book about Cleaning?

Simply because I wanted to encourage women in the life-giving beauty of homemaking without the guilt involved.

There are enough voices out there telling us to "just do it!" I am writing from the perspective of a woman who isn't a natural cleaner, but who wants to persevere in the traditions of homemaking. I do not believe homemaking is a dying art; rather, it is a time-tested skill that when cultivated creates a womb-like environment where life is nourished.

At its heart, *Having a Martha Home the Mary Way* is really about just that—the heart. *It is about releasing any personal guilt and shame you are carrying and embracing the truth that your "good enough" has nothing to do with your cleaning abilities.* Many of us need to hear that we don't have to get it all together to be good and loving. Our worth begins when we find our identity in the One who says, "By a single offering he has perfected for all time those who are being sanctified" (Hebrews 10:14, ESV).

I love the freedom that comes from knowing I am already—from eternity's perspective—perfect and complete, for all time. I don't have to do better or be better; I just need to walk faithfully with my God as He molds me.[1] And so do you.

You can keep and care for your home one step at a time, however imperfectly. You wear imperfect flesh, but you have a perfect soul if you know Him. The blood covers the ugly.

If you struggle with maintaining your house, you get overwhelmed, and you wish you had a maid (I'm praying for one for you!), don't let those feelings define you or get you stuck. Give them to God and walk in His steps as He goes before you.

I'm in this with you, and together, with Him and our hearts set on eternity, we can persevere!

What Does It Mean to Have a Martha House the Mary Way?

SUCH A FUN PLAY on words, isn't it? I wish it were my idea but I can't take the credit.

Before I wrote the first edition of this book, I had taken readers through a 31 Days to Clean blog series in which the biblical sisters Mary and Martha were not included. It was just me, offering encouragement to my readers before getting to the business of cleaning. However, when I decided to turn the blog series into an e-book, I asked my readers to help me come up with a subtitle. Beth Buster[1] brilliantly came up with *Having a Martha House the Mary Way*.

In the original e-book, I had meshed everything together but Christin Slade[2] encouraged me to make the Mary and Martha challenges separate from the main entry. These generous women helped shape the book into the inspiring resource you are holding in your hands. *Thank you both so much!*

And now, that subtitle (slightly tweaked) has become the title of this updated edition.

The Story of Mary and Martha

Now as they went on their way, Jesus entered a village. And a woman named Martha welcomed him into her house. And she had a sister called Mary, who sat at the Lord's feet and listened to his teaching. But Martha was distracted with much serving. And she went up to him and said, "Lord, do you not care that my sister has left me to serve alone? Tell her then to help me." But the Lord answered her, "Martha, Martha, you are anxious and troubled about many things, but one thing is necessary. Mary has chosen the good portion, which will not be taken away from her." LUKE 10:38-42, ESV

As I have studied the interactions between Martha and Mary, I have come not only to appreciate differences in personalities, but also to love the differences that make all of us who we are.

Some of us relate to Martha, the industrious, hardworking woman who is taking care of business, sometimes to the detriment of relationships. Some of us relate to Mary, the woman who would rather sit and be with the company than help with the work. There are admirable things about both of these women, but as we examine the story more closely, we can see how wise Mary's choices were. Let's look together.

Just for fun I decided to profile Mary and Martha, based on the accounts where they are mentioned—in Luke 10 above as well as John 11:1-44 and John 12:1-8. The profiles I've drawn up, though based on what we're told in the Bible, are expansions of my own perceptions of their personalities, so please keep that in mind.

Martha

It is a widely held belief that Martha is the older sister. It seems as though she has taken on the role of mother to her siblings, Mary and Lazarus, since no living parents are mentioned. She takes care of business, but it's evident that the weight of her family responsibilities is taking a toll on her. But that doesn't stop her. She is strong, keeps busy, and doesn't have time to mince words. She is bold, but sometimes forgets herself and doesn't always filter her responses. Martha doesn't seem to conform to the expectations of the culture, where women are submissive and quiet and know their place. She says what she thinks and can be demanding. She also knows when it's safe to be herself. She knows who Jesus is and has great faith in Him. But she is also troubled and anxious because she is the caretaker of the family; it hasn't quite sunk into her heart that God has promised and can be trusted to provide for them.

MARTHA'S KEY VERSES:

> *[Jesus said,] "Martha, Martha, you are anxious and troubled about many things, but one thing is necessary. Mary has chosen the good portion, which will not be taken away from her."* LUKE 10:41-42, ESV

Jesus said to [Martha], "I am the resurrection and the life. Whoever believes in me, though he die, yet shall he live, and everyone who lives and believes in me shall never die. Do you believe this?" She said to him, "Yes, Lord; I believe that you are the Christ, the Son of God, who is coming into the world."
JOHN 11:25-27, ESV

Jesus said, "Take away the stone." Martha, the sister of the dead man, said to him, "Lord, by this time there will be an odor, for he has been dead four days." JOHN 11:39, ESV

Mary

Mary, the apparent younger sister, is quiet and patient and exhibits great self-control. She wants to learn, and ponders what she hears. She understands what it means to be in the presence of Jesus, and she doesn't take it for granted. Mary allows herself to be vulnerable, and she is filled up inside with emotion, which she releases at the proper time. She is wise and faithful, and she knows what really matters. Her heart is laid bare, and she doesn't care who sees because she just wants Jesus.

MARY'S KEY VERSES:

Mary . . . sat at the Lord's feet and listened to his teaching. LUKE 10:39, ESV

[Jesus said,] "Martha, Martha, you are anxious and troubled about many things, but one thing is necessary. Mary has chosen the good portion, which will not be taken away from her." LUKE 10:41-42, ESV

[Martha] went and called her sister Mary, saying in private, "The Teacher is here and is calling for you." And when [Mary] heard it, she rose quickly and went to him. . . . Now when Mary came to where Jesus was and saw him, she fell at his feet, saying to him, "Lord, if you had been here, my brother would not have died." When Jesus saw her weeping, and the Jews who had come with her also weeping, he was deeply moved in his spirit. JOHN 11:28-29, 32-33, ESV

Mary therefore took a pound of expensive ointment made from pure nard, and anointed the feet of Jesus and wiped his feet with her hair. The house was filled with the fragrance of the perfume. JOHN 12:3, ESV

I can't wait to meet these women in heaven one day! What a joy it will be to truly get to know them.

Here's the lovely thing we learn from John's Gospel: "Now Jesus *loved* Martha and her sister and Lazarus" (John 11:5, emphasis added). That fact is evident through all of these Scripture snapshots, both in Jesus' words and His actions toward them. Jesus loved these women. He loved their whole family.

And so it is with us. We don't have to have a certain "right" personality to be loved. Jesus loves us as we are. But one way He shows His love to us is to uncover us, because He sees into the deep places where our wounds and worries are hidden. He knows each one of them, and He wants us to be free from their grip and be whole.

As we go through these next thirty-one days, I want you to love who you are and yet be able to let Jesus into the hard places. I want you to sit with Him and let Him heal you, so you can be whole.

This is why there are Mary and Martha challenges. First, we get our hearts right before the Lord, and then we can tackle the practical business.

So yes, let's work toward having a Martha-like home, but let's do it the Mary way, with our hearts focused first on Jesus. May we begin each day with this prayer: "My choice is you, GOD, first and only" (Psalm 16:5, MSG).

My Story

IT WAS DARK AND we were in the car outside of an ice cream shop. Tears were fresh on my cheeks. My sister-in-law, Renee, and I had set out to pick up some milk, but more was to come out of that trip than picking up a few gallons of dairy products.

I was crying because my heart hurt deeply; the feelings of not being a good enough wife were eating me up, and I didn't know what to do. I told my sister-in-law that I thought my husband, Jesse, would rather be married to someone else, someone better, who was good at cleaning. "I have this friend," I said through my tears, "who gets up early, is efficient, and is so good at cleaning and getting things done. I'm sure Jesse wishes I was like her. I'm such a failure."

As Renee began to speak life-giving truth to me, my mind raced, trying to rewind the events that had brought me to this point of brokenness and disappointment in myself.

An Inclination toward Messy . . .
Plus Babies and Aprons

Nearly all of my childhood, after my parents divorced, I lived with my dad and stepmom. My stepmom cleaned everything except my room; I never even washed a dish. In fact, I didn't do my own laundry until I was fourteen and living with my mom.

Under my dad's roof, I was expected to keep my room fairly clean. If I let it get too messy, I would find a note from him on my bed saying something like, "YOU MAY NOT GO TO YOUNG LIFE OR DO ANYTHING UNTIL THIS ROOM IS CLEAN. Love, Dad." He rarely came down hard on me, but he did want me to take care of my room. When I moved in with my mom, it was a whole new ball game. I could keep my room in whatever state I liked; my mom didn't care about it at all. I had freedom! I don't think I was terribly messy, but I didn't put much stock in tidy surroundings.

Once I got to college, my true colors really came out. I roomed with a gal who was extremely neat, and it became clear immediately that I wasn't. I remember her actually taking tape and creating a line midway across the top of the vanity between her side and mine so my mess wouldn't creep over to her organized side. She was mostly gracious, but I'm pretty sure I drove her crazy.

The next place I lived, I had another roommate who kept things spotless, and again, I had to work hard to do my part. Finally, my junior year, I moved in with a gal who was just like me, if not worse. Our one-bedroom apartment always looked like a bomb had gone off in it.

One morning while we were still in our beds, we heard the front door to our apartment open. We looked at each other, and then my roomie threw the covers over her head thinking that it would be a cue for the unexpected visitor to go away. I started to get my defensive hackles up when all of a sudden we heard, "Ahhh . . . ohhh . . . uhhh . . . groan." *What in the world?*

I opened our bedroom door to find our landlady bleeding on the bathroom floor, in a pile of our mess. She had tripped over our clutter in the hallway, veered off, and hit her head on the bathroom sink. Talk about embarrassing! She was there for some sort of routine maintenance check, which apparently we had been advised of in a mailed notice that was most certainly in the papers strewn all over the floor. If I had known of the upcoming visit by actually reading the paper, I would have cleaned up a bit. Really.

Of course, the upside for my roomie and me was the assurance that if someone did decide to break into the apartment, the intruder would probably end up in a bloody heap before doing any harm.

Fast-forward to my first year of marriage. Jesse and I lived in the small apartment that my messy roomie and I had shared—she had moved out and I stayed. I tried to keep it nice for my husband. My biggest issue was papers and junk that all ended up on the dining room table. And I always had a messy kitchen. But still, in my opinion, it wasn't too terrible. My husband and I were stretching into our new lives together, learning about each other, and just enjoying the freedom that marriage brings. It wasn't until I got pregnant that things got ugly really fast.

Along with the surprising and exciting news that I was pregnant, I also got incredibly sick. I threw up from morning to night, had terrible headaches from not getting enough food, and one evening ended up becoming so dehydrated that I was taken to the hospital and hooked up to an IV. I couldn't go to work, and I was in bed most of the day hitting myself in the head with the palms of my hands (like that helped), wishing for a narcotic to knock me out for three months. No such narcotic arrived. When I would feel hungry or get a craving, I had just enough strength to half-crawl to the kitchen, eat a few bites, throw up, and go back to bed.

Jesse was a senior in college at the time, and when he would come home from class, the apartment was littered with bowls and cups that I had brought out but not put back in the kitchen. The place was a wreck, and I'm sure the smell wasn't too pleasant. My husband was carrying a full course load plus an internship with a police department so he not only had to study for his classes, but many times he was pulling overnight third-shift hours required for the internship. He was exhausted and overloaded, and I was exhausted and sick.

He resented me for not taking the dishes to the kitchen, and I resented him for not understanding how terrible I felt with my pregnancy. Just the thought of moving made me queasy. He thought I was exaggerating, and I thought he was not supportive. Our marriage went through a really rough time during the initial months of my first pregnancy.

Unfortunately, my next two pregnancies weren't any better. I was nauseous all the time, the house was a wreck, and the bitterness between us was becoming worse. It was awful.

I would try to establish a routine, but of course as soon as I did, I would have another baby, or one of my children would go through a change (teething, crawling, etc.) that wrecked my routine. Or I was just exhausted from getting up at night, nursing, and caring for three little ones. I struggled with motivation, fatigue, laziness, lack of self-discipline, and constant feelings of failure and guilt. I sincerely wanted to be a good wife and homemaker, but I felt that I was failing miserably.

So I tried harder.

I read everything on cleaning and being a good wife and mother. I perused the Internet for tips and tricks, and read all about biblical womanhood. Oh yes, I would be that woman, that biblical, godly woman who cared for her home, her husband, and her children no matter what; all my energies would go toward the goal of making my home a haven. I even invested in pretty aprons.

But then I ended up in the car outside the ice cream shop.

What Went Wrong?

My heart was in the right place, and I had good ideals. I wanted to care for my home and my family, but those ideals weren't translating into my everyday life. I knew I needed God to intervene.

But there was pain before there was peace.

That night in the car, I just felt weighed down. I had convinced myself I couldn't change, so why bother? I bared my soul to my sister-in-law: "Jesse would be happier with someone other than me. My kids deserve a better mother, one who can at least keep the house clean." I began to feel that my worth as a person was reflected in windows that sparkled and floors that glistened.

"Has Jesse ever said that he wants a different wife?" my sister-in-law asked.

"Well, no," I admitted.

She looked me right in the eyes and said, "No one has the authority to tell you who you are. Not your husband, not anyone. Only God has the authority to tell you who you are."

And just like a hammer crashing into a glass window, she shattered the lie that my worth was determined by my cleaning abilities.

It slowly sank in. *I don't define who I am, cleaning doesn't define who I am, my husband doesn't define who I am, certain ideas of biblical womanhood don't define who I am* [although I didn't realize that last one until later]*; only God can tell me who I am.* I wasn't exactly sure who that was yet (that's been a process), but I knew that I would no longer equate my identity with cleaning.

I would be free from that burden.

It took a while to break clean of the habit of defining

myself that way. From time to time, I still reverted to feelings of worthlessness, but God put a stop to that in October 2010.

I don't know how or why or what the circumstance was, but somehow this revelation went straight to my heart from the Holy Spirit.

I am clay, and clay cannot mold itself.

No matter how much I try or strive or work hard at becoming better or good enough, I can't do it. Only He can work with this clay woman. So I throw my hands up and submit, trusting His work in my life.

No More Striving

> *O LORD, You are our Father,*
> *We are the clay, and You our potter;*
> *And all of us are the work of Your hand.*
> ISAIAH 64:8

As the verse says, we all are clay.

It's humbling to realize that there are some issues in our lives we can't change on our own, the ones that we can't seem to overcome no matter how hard we try; we must consciously be willing to let the Holy Spirit step in. But it's important to recognize that how we live every day—the choices we make—should be done with discernment, listening to the Father through His Word and the Holy Spirit. It's how we grow up and mature. And who does the maturing? Who sanctifies us, matures us to be more like Jesus?

*I will not presume to speak of anything except what
Christ has accomplished through me.* ROMANS 15:18

*Christ also loved the church and gave Himself up for
her, so that He might sanctify her, having cleansed
her by the washing of water with the word, that He
might present to Himself the church in all her glory,
having no spot or wrinkle or any such thing; but that
she would be holy and blameless.*
EPHESIANS 5:25-27

*Now may the God of peace Himself sanctify you
entirely.* 1 THESSALONIANS 5:23

*We should always give thanks to God for you . . .
because God has chosen you from the beginning for
salvation through sanctification by the Spirit and
faith in the truth.* 2 THESSALONIANS 2:13

*To those who . . . are chosen according to the
foreknowledge of God the Father, by the sanctifying
work of the Spirit.* 1 PETER 1:1-2

Christ's death on the cross and His resurrection began our
sanctification, and it is the Holy Spirit in us who continues
the work that works out our salvation! It is the treasure that
was given to us when we believed. He does the work; He
matures us. What a freeing revelation that we can't do it, but
that the Holy Spirit can, in His power and strength.

Christ did the work on the cross. The Holy Spirit continues the work in our lives. Our job? To surrender to Him and walk faithfully one day at a time.

Surrendering in Real Life

How does this surrender and belief that the Holy Spirit is doing the work in me play out in everyday life? What does it look like practically?

For me, it's like this:

I *live*.

I get up, I work, I enjoy, I trust. I still live on this earth and I am able to walk through this life with great freedom. I am in God's will right now, in this moment, and so I'm no longer worried about every step I take. I am doing what the Bible calls "walking by faith."

> *We walk by faith, not by sight.*
> 2 CORINTHIANS 5:7

I watch for evidence of God around me, and I listen to Him through His Word. I go forward with my days, knowing that He will direct my steps. I can't really go wrong if I'm walking by faith, and if I do, I know He will use it for His good plan.

The biggest part of living out of faith and belief in the work of the Spirit is that I do not focus on my ability or inability to do this or that. I do what I can as I can.

I wash my sheets. I do the dishes. When I don't do the

laundry or the dishes, I don't allow the lie *I'm no good* to interfere. Instead, I remember that I am human. Which means I'm going to mess up and fail, but I'm not a failure. I'm literally a work in progress. And I accept that.

I accept that some days I will get lazy and make big mistakes and fall. But I will go to the throne of grace and receive the truth that I am still a new creation in Christ. I am new because of Christ, not by anything I can do or did do. I am because He is.

So I walk, I fall; I walk, I fall; and all along I am available for Him to mold.

I believe in His work on my good days and my worst days.

So whether the dishes or laundry get done or not, I am secure in the fact that I am who God says I am.

I want to work hard and take care of my family and my home, and I'm doing so every day, knowing I am free and I am loved.

As you read this book, I want you to take whatever fears, failures, insecurities, and any other issues that are balled up like a fist inside you, and place them in your hand. Now open your hand and release them to God, letting Him take them and show you a new way.

You are so loved. I can't wait for you to see how He shows you that over and over during the next few weeks.

How to Use This Book

I KNOW THAT NONE of us live in identical houses with the same number of family members and cleaning challenges. You might be a single woman in a one-bedroom apartment, and another reader might be in a six-bedroom home with ten children. I based the cleaning schedule on the average house: three bedrooms, two bathrooms, a living room, kitchen, and dining room. There are days to clean a family room, an office, and a homeschool space, as well as a project day to clean another area that I didn't list. I would like you to implement the cleaning ideas Monday through Friday, use Saturday for projects you need to catch up on or for extra rooms, and reserve Sunday for rest.

Feel free to adjust and make the plan work for you. Let's say you have a basement instead of a family room. Just use the family room day to work on the basement. See how flexible it is?

Each day there is a reading designed to encourage you, inspire you, get you thinking, and get you energized. There is no judgment; this isn't boot camp. Come as you are and have some fun as you make your surroundings sparkle and infuse your heart and your home with peace.

After the day's reading, you will be given two challenges: a Mary Challenge and a Martha Challenge. The Mary Challenge speaks to your heart and the Martha Challenge spurs you to action.

My goal is to inspire you and give practical help to get you moving and cleaning, so that ultimately your house will be nice and tidy by the end of the thirty-one days.

But of course it isn't just about the cleaning.

My hope is that through the readings and the Mary Challenges, you will be motivated and also be able to experience peace throughout the process. I want to engage your heart, and I want you to have rest in your soul.

The world needs both Marys and Marthas, and if we can embrace a little of both of them, I think we'll grasp this homemaking thing with gumption and grace.

 ## Mary Challenges ·

Through the Mary Challenges, I want to encourage you to get rest and fill your heart with God's peace by sitting with the Lord, reading the Scriptures, and learning from Him. In fact, when we choose to sit with Jesus first, we are choosing the "good portion" that Mary did while Martha was bustling around trying to get everything accomplished.

Before the cleaning and the day with all of its (possible) troubles gets ahold of you (Matthew 6:34), I'm encouraging you to get ahold of Him.

These challenges will get you pondering different aspects of your life and offer you practical ideas to inspire you over the next few weeks.

Martha Challenges ——————————————

The Martha Challenges are designed for those of us who are not born cleaners. Oh, we want a clean home, and we start out with good intentions, but we tend to get overwhelmed with ALL THERE IS TO DO because we aren't consistent with keeping on top of the cleaning. *Ahem.* The Martha Challenges in this book break down cleaning tasks into manageable steps for you, spreading them out over a month. These are not deep-cleaning tasks; these are let's-get-this-house-in-order tasks. Hence, there are no challenges to dust the ceilings or rotate mattresses. While those tasks are worthwhile for keeping a home in clean shape, this book does not go into that depth. However, we *will* organize junk drawers and scrub toilets.

Getting Your Kids Involved and Bonus Tips

Some days include a section called Get Your Kids Involved! This is for those of you who have children and want to utilize their capabilities. Directing their exuberance and energy into hands-on responsibility is a boon for all of you. Never underestimate how much your kids are able to do. The Bonus Tips are extra tips to help you for that particular day to hopefully make your cleaning life easier!

Are you ready? Let's get to it!

DAY 0

Prep Day!

The secret of getting ahead is getting started.

MARK TWAIN

THIS IS YOUR GET-AHEAD-BEFORE-YOU-BEGIN day. You will need to pick a day that you can spend a few hours cleaning. For many of you, this will be a Saturday.

Your job: Get the kitchen and main spaces clean so you can begin the full challenge with a clean slate. This isn't the time for deep cleaning; it's just a general pickup and getting your kitchen clean (dishes washed, floor swept). Think simple! For me, if I take a few hours and just get to work, I can get so much accomplished, and that sets me up for success during the busy weekdays.

I have found that if I'm going to be digging into cleaning

and purging throughout my whole house, I need to have a fresh start in my main living spaces or I feel too overwhelmed. Plus, you will have more momentum if you start ahead of the game.

SUPPLY LIST

Here is a list of supplies you want to make sure you have on hand as you begin:

- ☐ Sponges and/or cleaning rags
- ☐ Mop
- ☐ Broom and hand broom
- ☐ All-purpose cleaner
- ☐ Floor cleaners (for wood, vinyl)
- ☐ Wood cleaner (for dusting)
- ☐ Toilet bowl brush
- ☐ Toilet bowl cleaner
- ☐ All-purpose bathroom cleaner
- ☐ Tile and tub cleaner
- ☐ Glass cleaner

DAY 1

Lifting Life above Mere Existence

Life-giving is about receiving from God in order to give to others.
BARBARA MOUSER, *Five Aspects of Woman*

TUCKED INTO A MOUNTAINTOP, surrounded by trees and blue skies, her home sat waiting to greet me. As I approached her door, I saw a sign on the side of the house that said, "Welcome, Sarah! We are so glad you are here!" Through the front door, into the entryway, I was greeted with smiles and hugs. After introductions, I was shown to my room where I would be staying for the next few days.

Next to the neatly made bed was a bottle of water, a vase of simple flowers, a beautifully handwritten note, and a little jar of foil-wrapped chocolates.

This lovely setup, personally arranged, was all for *me*.

Back upstairs, the smell of a homemade meal was floating in the air. Candles were lit and classical music was playing in the background.

This was my first time to visit the home of my mentor. I had flown hundreds of miles to visit her, to spend time with her family, and to be mentored by her in person. And immediately upon pulling up to her home, I felt so special, so loved.

I would have been happy just to be there with her without any of the extras, but she chose to make things beautiful for me. Going the extra step to raise life above mere existence is her defining gift.

I want to do that also—to be someone who takes the time to make the ordinary into something beautiful.

Because we are created to be life-givers.

All women are life-givers; God made us that way. Life-giving, in its most basic sense, is raising life above the level of mere existence. We give life physically and spiritually, in many forms. We also give life intellectually, socially, and artistically. We as women have been blessed with the very nature of life-giving! At its core, life-giving is all about love— loving others with what God has given us.

Just think of it: Our bodies hold and nurture life as a baby grows within, and then we are able to hold and nurture life with our hands and our minds and our creativity—to live life and make it lovely and vibrant for the world around us. What a gift!

You can give life to your home by making it warm and inviting, fresh and invigorating! You can give life to your home by making sure there are clean dishes to eat off of and clear spaces to walk in and organized papers that are easy to find when you need them. You can give life to your home by filling it with loving, true, and good words! You can give life to your home by building up the souls in your care and the souls who enter it. Your home can be a place where weary bones rest and burdens are lifted and laughter ripples through every room. All of these things make a home.

You are a creator of beauty and peace and safe spaces.

You are a homemaker.

Let's embrace this empowering definition of who we are: "Who is woman? She is the redeemed life-giver, enlivened by the love of Christ and continuously renewed by Him as she nurtures others."[1]

Mary Challenge

READ DEUTERONOMY 30:15-16 ·················

What does God say about choosing life or death?

Why do we choose life? Do you think it's more than just physical life we choose? Why?

Have you looked at yourself as a life-giver, as someone who can choose to raise life above mere existence?

_____

_____

_____

_____

_____

Think of some ways you can bring life into your home. What are some things that would make you smile to see or experience in your home?

_____

_____

_____

_____

What can you do today to raise life above mere existence?

_____

_____

_____

MARTHA CHALLENGE

 Put a load of laundry in the wash.

CLEAN YOUR KITCHEN.

DO THE DISHES

1. First, do the dishes. *Give a WOOT if you have a dishwasher and praise the Lord for it!*

2. Also the pans—yes, even the greasy piled-up ones you haven't wanted to touch.

3. Wash out the sink. (If you have bleach, plug your sink and fill it with water, add a dash of bleach, and let it sit for half an hour.)

NEXT, GATHER UP ALL THE PAPERWORK

4. Gather up all the paperwork, junk mail, and stuff on your counters, put it in a bin or a bag, and set it aside. You'll deal with this on another day.

5. Wipe down the counters.

6. Eat a cookie.

Every morning during this challenge I want you to clean the kitchen. Yes, every morning. YOU CAN DO IT! I'm with you, sister. Oh, and by "clean the kitchen," I just mean the dishes and the surface areas.

 Put the laundry in the dryer.

GET YOUR KIDS INVOLVED!

Mobilize your kids to help! My five-year-old loves to wash the pans because to her, it's fun! Crazy, right? Just go with it. Give your kiddo the soap and a scrubby, and let your helper go to town on the pans. Don't hover—let it be. I promise the pans will be cleaner than they were before—they might even get completely clean!

BONUS TIP

Put your dishes on a lower shelf so your child can put the dishes away *and* set the table easily. My kids have been unloading the dishwasher since each of them was four years old. They can do it!

DAY 2

Define Your Vision

Where there is no vision, the people are unrestrained.

PROVERBS 29:18

SITTING IN MY FAVORITE comfy brown chair, I look around and I begin to *feel* what I see.

Chaos.

Toys and books and a blanket and papers and disheveled pillows and a few dirty cups—it all feels like too much. I am trying to write, but I can't block out the mess I see; the mess makes its way into my spirit, and my mind can't focus.

I need clarity and peace and space to think, both physically and mentally. When there is a mess swirling around me on the outside, I internalize it. For me, chaos outside equals chaos inside.

This isn't going to work. I need to take a few minutes to straighten up.

I get up and begin by neatly placing the pillows on my couch. Ah, much better. I gather the toys and throw them into my kids' rooms—we'll deal with that mess later. Trash in the trash can, papers scooped up into piles and bagged, set out of sight for now. Books piled onto shelves and dirty cups taken to the kitchen.

I light a candle and put on some soothing music.

Now I'm ready to begin. Now I can think.

Only one small problem: On the edges of my mind I know the mess is still there, hiding just around the corner. While I'm able to focus better than I was before, the mess is still tugging at me.

I realize that in order for me to have a clear mind, I need a clear space. I need a space that brings me peace instead of chaos, clarity instead of clutter.

Is it just me who feels this way? No, I know my husband, Jesse, doesn't like a mess. My daughter Caroline tells me sometimes, "When I have a home, I'll keep it clean and organized." Yep, it gets to her, too. I begin to have a new resolve to keep my home clean; I want to give myself and my family peace of mind, and clear, clean, inviting spaces to think and do and live.

I am motivated by a desire to create a peaceful home for the people I love.

So here's my question to you: Why do *you* want a clean home?

That may sound like a silly question, but I think it's important that you discover for yourself why you want a clean home. I'm not just talking about the need to keep the roaches away. If you do not own your reasons, if you do not have *vision*, you will be unmotivated and quite frankly bored with the whole idea of persevering in cleaning. However, if you can name it, you can claim it; you can and will be much more motivated to keep going toward your goal.

I believe if you can generate a list of the whys, then you will be able to look at them and remind yourself day in and day out why you are spending time on the mundane activities that never seem to stay accomplished. You need to have purpose in what you're doing; you need vision, or you will continue to stay in a rut. Once you figure out the why, you will already be one step ahead of yourself.

You want to know why I clean? Why I push through the mundane, even though I really dislike it and would rather do just about anything else?

I hang on to my resolve in cleaning for these three main reasons:

1. I need a safe, sanitary, peaceable environment for my family.
2. I want to love myself and others well.
3. I am becoming like Jesus.

1. A SAFE, SANITARY, PEACEABLE ENVIRONMENT

I love going to hotels. I love the clean sheets and towels, the coffee cups set out just waiting for me to fill them, the cozy couch with one pillow sitting in the middle of it, the desk that is clean from clutter, and especially the room service (cleaning and food). I feel so pampered when I can stay in a nice hotel. The staff wants to please me, and it's their job to make sure my room is clean and cozy.

I'm not running a hotel at my house, but I am trying to create an environment that is clean and makes whoever is in my home feel cared for in serene surroundings. Our homes should be places of refuge. I want my family to have warm memories about their home. I want them to live in an environment that is healthy, safe, and super cozy. I want all these things because I love myself and my family.

2. LOVING MYSELF AND OTHERS WELL

For me, the heart of cleaning has everything to do with loving people well. The house I live in might not be eternal, but the people in it certainly are. So how can I take this non-eternal structure and create a life-giving, eternal atmosphere? I can use the house to create a home. I can offer my family, my friends, myself, and even strangers the gift of love by making them feel special when they are in my home. I can do this by keeping it clean, making it pleasing to the eye, offering comfortable spaces to relax (put your feet up!), and turning it into a place where I serve others. In the serving and intentional care, I can love well.

3. BECOMING LIKE JESUS

After I graduated from Penn State University, I worked at a crisis pregnancy clinic as a counselor and an abstinence presentation manager. But you know what I had to do sometimes? I had to scrub the kitchen floor. I resented my boss for making me do these "lower" jobs. *I'm not getting paid to scrub floors,* I thought. *I am getting paid to help women and high school students make wise decisions.* Okay, it's pretty evident that I was reacting immaturely, even though I didn't realize it at the time. Little did I know that my boss was teaching me to be like Jesus. Jesus didn't grasp His equality with God; He chose instead to be a servant—to be humble and to offer Himself to do His Father's will.

When I enter into the mundane and choose to clean even when I don't want to, I am closer to who Jesus is. I am choosing to be like Him. And when this happens, not only is my character changing for the better, but cleaning becomes an act of worship.

I know I will never be awesome at cleaning, and I'm completely fine with that. I know who I am and I am content in my own skin. But I do want to at least have a comfortable, peaceful environment to retreat to, not only for myself but for my family.

So, what's your why?

Mary Challenge

 READ PROVERBS 14:1 ····························

In order to build, we need a plan, and for a plan, we need vision.

Identify specific reasons—your vision—for why you want to have a clean home, and then complete a mission statement based on those reasons. Maybe your mission will be in the form of a paragraph, a poem, or a list. Consider adding a Scripture verse or a quote that motivates you. You can begin jotting down your ideas on the lines provided, then use a separate piece of paper for the final draft.

_____

_____

_____

_____

_____

_____

_____

_____

_____

_____

_____

_____

_____

_____

_____

When you are finished, it should take you no longer than a minute to read over your mission statement. Now dress it up, make it pretty, and put it in a frame if you'd like! Be creative and have fun! Put it somewhere where you can see it every day.

 **MARTHA CHALLENGE**

We're back in the kitchen!

TODAY, LET'S TAKE ON THE FRIDGE AND THE MICROWAVE.

 FIRST, THE FRIDGE

1. Open it up. Thank the Lord for the abundance of food you have and for making so much of it taste good.

2. Then begin purging. Get rid of anything that has expired or is old or has things growing on it or is smelly.

3. Once that's done, remove everything and wash down the interior.

4. Now organize and put your food back into the fridge. Breathe a deep sigh of joy. Your fridge is clean. Praise the Lord!

 NEXT, THE MICROWAVE

5. Put some sliced lemons in a bowl of water and microwave it for two to three minutes. This will help loosen up any food crusted or stuck inside.

6. Then wash it down and get her clean! Don't forget to wash the exterior.

BONUS TIP

While you're in the kitchen, put a sheet of aluminum foil on the bottom rack of your oven to catch any grease when you're cooking. Make sure it is on the rack, not the bottom surface of the oven. It will save you *so* much cleaning time later!

DAY 3

Rhythm Priorities

Rhythm is very individual. You can't impose a rhythm on somebody; you have to enter into a rhythm. And people don't have to have the same rhythm. . . . Find the rhythm of your own body, your own life, your own history. . . . Live out who you are in relationship to who God is, who Jesus is.

EUGENE PETERSON

IT'S MIDNIGHT, AND IT'S happening again.

My heart feels heavy inside my chest, and my mind is in overdrive. I'm thinking about all the things I need to do to make sure I am raising my children well. I need to make sure I'm teaching them and preparing them for life.

I'm thinking about all my failures and the weight of my responsibilities. More thoughts push their way in. *I need to get my home in order. I need to write my friend back. I need to turn in that article. I need to set aside time for my husband.*

I don't want to drop the ball, *not again*. But there are so many balls, and I'm not good at juggling. I just want to sleep . . .

Have you ever experienced anxiety that is triggered by all you have to do? When it hits me, it hits hard. But I'm learning to embrace the anxiety and let it be a teacher instead of a master.

Learning from Anxiety and Finding Rhythm

There is an ebb and flow to life, a rhythm, and even though we put things in order, life isn't exactly a straight line. When we're talking about priorities, it's easy to divvy things up into a numerical order, but as life shifts and stretches, our circumstances may cause the order to move and change. Nonetheless, I think it is profitable to prioritize how we want to live so we can keep a pulse on how we're doing, but I find that life is more in sync with rhythms than with straight-line priorities.

With that said, let's talk about priorities and our rhythms.

If you're anything like me, you have good intentions but you often fall short. For example, I always say God is first in my life, but is my life reflecting that? Do I spend time with the Lord each day? What does my prayer life look like? How much time is spent on hiding God's Word in my heart? You can see where I'm going with this. It's easy to say what our priorities are, but it's not always easy to live them out.

With God's grace and light to lead us, we can live out our rhythm priorities without shame or fear of failure.

We offer ourselves to God and ask His Spirit to help us, and then we walk into our days the best we can. Some days we're limping, and some days we're leaping, but we can always keep our heads high, turned toward the heavens, relying on the love from our Father to walk with us through the day. We are never alone.

Here are some priorities I hold close:

TIME WITH GOD

I want to be in communion with Him daily so I can keep on in His love and continue to grow, as the Word intersects with the Holy Spirit in me, maturing and helping me.

My work-in-progress goal

Spend time in the Word every morning, sometime before the day carries me away. If this doesn't happen, I'll read in the afternoon or when I have a few moments of quiet.

Verses to motivate me

His delight is in the law of the LORD,
And in His law he meditates day and night.
He will be like a tree firmly planted by streams of water,
Which yields its fruit in its season
And its leaf does not wither;
And in whatever he does, he prospers.

PSALM 1:2-3

In the morning I will order my prayer to You
and eagerly watch.

PSALM 5:3

Seek first His kingdom and His righteousness, and all
these things will be added to you. MATTHEW 6:33

In the early morning, while it was still dark, Jesus got up, left the house, and went away to a secluded place, and was praying there. MARK 1:35

MY HUSBAND
I want to be a faithful, life-giving wife, bringing help, comfort, and companionship to my husband. I want to be his biggest fan and his best friend.

My work-in-progress goal
Be quicker to listen and slower to speak. Be kind. Cuddle with him more.

 ## Verses to motivate me ....

Her husband can trust her,
*   and she will greatly enrich his life.*
She brings him good, not harm,
*   all the days of her life.*
PROVERBS 31:11-12, NLT

Two are better than one because they have a good return for their labor. For if either of them falls, the one will lift up his companion. ECCLESIASTES 4:9-10

MY CHILDREN
My kids are my best buds. I love them and who God made them to be, and I am so thankful they are mine to raise. What a gift!

My goal is to love them well, show them grace and compassion, and instill in them truth and goodness and beauty.

I also want to teach my children how to behave because they will grow up and be a part of the world, and I want them to know how to act and love and contribute worthwhile things. I want them to shine with God's light so they can be a part of bringing God's Kingdom to bear on the earth. All of these lessons take time and intention. I also want to just have fun with them! Life is too short not to laugh and play.

My work-in-progress goal
Become more consistent in my cleaning so I can be freed up to spend time with the kiddos, not worrying about all I need to do. Bring them alongside me so they can learn to take care of their home as well. We are a team!

Verses to motivate me

Write these commandments that I've given you today on your hearts. Get them inside of you and then get them inside your children. Talk about them wherever you are, sitting at home or walking in the street; talk about them from the time you get up in the morning to when you fall into bed at night. Tie them on your hands and foreheads as a reminder; inscribe them on the doorposts of your homes and on your city gates.

DEUTERONOMY 6:7-8, MSG

Train up a child in the way he should go;
even when he is old he will not depart from it.

PROVERBS 22:6, ESV

MY HOME

I want a clean home, not a perfect home. I want to create an inviting place of comfort and peace. I want a place where my family feels secure and at rest.

My work-in-progress goal

Clean the kitchen every morning. When the kitchen is clean, I feel like I can take on anything!

📖 Verses to motivate me ·····················

The wise woman builds her house,
But the foolish tears it down with her own hands.

PROVERBS 14:1

She looks well to the ways of her household,
And does not eat the bread of idleness.

PROVERBS 31:27

Do all things without grumbling.

PHILIPPIANS 2:14

Whatever you do, do your work heartily,
as for the Lord rather than for men.

COLOSSIANS 3:23

MY GIFTS

I want to nurture and use my God-given gifts and talents to strengthen the church and be a light to the world around me.

My work-in-progress goal

Use my words carefully. Focus on loving and giving grace through my verbal and written words.

📖 Verses to motivate me ·················

> As each one has received a special gift, employ it in serving one another as good stewards of the manifold grace of God. I PETER 4:10

PERSONAL

I want to carve out time to enjoy life and spend time with friends!

My work-in-progress goal

Take the time to read good books, write in my journal, and spend time with friends over delicious food.

📖 Verses to motivate me ·················

> Day by day continuing with one mind in the temple, and breaking bread from house to house, they were taking their meals together with gladness and sincerity of heart, praising God and having favor with all the people. ACTS 2:46-47

{ *Mary Challenge* }

 READ MATTHEW 22:37-40 ························

What is the most important focus we should have as we go about our days?

_____

_____

_____

_____

Come up with a list of your priorities, but don't number them. Write them down on the lines provided. Ask the Lord for the grace to keep them as best you can, and to begin again when you mess up. Each day is full of His mercies;[1] let's not waste any of them by beating ourselves up.

_____

_____

_____

_____

_____

_____

_____

MARTHA CHALLENGE

We are still in the kitchen (and still doing laundry)! For the love, let's get it done.

TODAY WE ARE TACKLING THE FLOOR AND THE OUTSIDE OF THE CABINETS.

 THE CABINETS

1. That's right, it's time to sweep and scrub those floors, but first, the cabinets.

2. Take a close look at the cabinet doors. Do you see the grime and stuck-on food? Go on, grab your sponge and get to work! And when you finish with the cabinets . . .

MOVE ON TO THE FLOOR

3. Do not even look at a handheld mop. Oh no, sister, you need a sponge or cleaning rag, a scrub brush, and a bucket full of hot soapy water. Get on your hands and knees. (If you use a gardening kneeling pad, it's a tad more comfortable.) Clean those floors well! Attack those dried-up pieces of mac 'n' cheese, the dust-covered Cheerio, and the . . . *what is that*? Get it too! Scrub, baby, scrub!

👪 *GET YOUR KIDS INVOLVED!*

How about asking your child to help you? Give your recruit the sponge and the soapy water and let him or her wash the floors. I would have an older child (over six) do this, unless you want water everywhere (ask me how I know).

PAY YOUR CHILD

You could offer to pay your child to help if this is not one of his or her everyday chores. Fifty cents sounds about right for the floor and fifty cents for the cabinets. What do you think?

I don't know about you, but I'll take all the help I can get!

There is a time for everything,
and a season for every activity under the heavens.

ECCLESIASTES 3:1, NIV

DAY 4

Developing a Workable Routine

Anchors bring order to your day.

SALLY CLARKSON

IT'S A DAY MY kids and I always look forward to: the spring day we pull the big white poster board out from behind our homeschool buffet cabinet and start planning.

"It's time to make our summer schedule," I say. I begin writing out what our days will look like over the months of sunshine and freedom from a full school load. After I finish a basic, bare-bones routine, I ask my children to make it pretty. With markers in hand, they go to work, coloring and adding pictures.

Once we are finished, we hang it in our dining room for all to see. Let the summer days begin!

Do you have a schedule—a schedule that you actually *follow* every day? Or do you like to create schedules but never get around to following them?

I am in the latter category.

I love to write schedules and make little plans for myself, but following them is, well, not my best strength. In order to remedy this fault of mine (and yes, I consider it a fault), I have decided to come up with a routine (not a schedule) that fits my God-given nature. It must be flexible, easy, and workable.

I want you to do the same.

Are you up for the challenge?

For those of you who hate the word *schedule*, please don't brush me off! I am not suggesting you pencil in something for every minute of the day (or even hour, for that matter). What I'm going to suggest is coming up with a plan (routine, mama's workable day, whatever you want to call it) that works for you.

Creating a Workable Schedule
REVIEW YOUR RHYTHM PRIORITIES

If you haven't written down your rhythm priorities yet, get to it! They will give your schedule an overall direction. What are you trying to accomplish? What priority needs more time and what needs less? Has something that isn't on your list taken over? If your priorities are to keep your house in order and pay attention to your kiddos, but you find yourself on the computer more often than not, you may have to rethink when you do this so it doesn't interfere with the items you have identified as deserving precedence. Maybe setting a time limit on the computer for yourself would help.

THINK IN TERMS OF ANCHORS

I learned this principle from my mentor, Sally Clarkson. What consistent routines or anchors can you put in your day to keep things on track? For example, in my house, one of the anchors for my kids and me is 2:00 p.m. teatime. We stop what we're doing, make tea and a snack, gather pillows and blankets, and head to the living room for reading and tea. The most common anchors that people have are set times for breakfast, lunch, and dinner. For moms of little ones, nap time certainly is an anchor. Figure out the anchors that provide stability for your family.

MAKE SURE TO SCHEDULE TIME FOR YOUR HOBBIES

Whether your favorite hobbies include blogging, reading, writing, scrapbooking, or something else, intentionally make time for them. Maybe you have only fifteen minutes a day to focus on a certain hobby, or maybe you can block out two hours. Whatever the case, use the time you've scheduled; otherwise you will probably end up wasting time or losing it altogether.

DO WHAT COMES NATURALLY

When creating your workable schedule, figure out what's already set in your day. What comes naturally to you? Start there and don't try to change it—just go with it. You will add on from there.

WRITE IT DOWN

You can be as detailed or as simple as you like. You can come up with a complete cleaning schedule with different things to do each day of the week or a general one. Either way, do what fits you. Then stick it somewhere you will see it every day. Yes, it can and will change—be flexible.

Mary Challenge

☕ **READ PROVERBS 24:27**

How does coming up with a doable routine compare with preparing a field before building a house?

_____

_____

_____

_____

Write out a realistic routine for your family (something basic) and put it in a place where everyone can see it. As you get used to the routine, talk together about amending or expanding it.

_____

_____

_____

_____

_____

_____

_____

_____

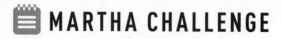

MARTHA CHALLENGE

TODAY, WE'RE CLEANING THE PANTRY.

As always, do what you can if you don't have time to complete the whole challenge. If you only have time to get rid of the expired items, that's an accomplishment in itself.

PULL OUT EVERYTHING

1. That's right, all of it. Depending on the size of your pantry, this job might take a half hour or up to two hours to complete.

THROW IT OUT

2. Check the items and throw out all the expired stuff. Make sure to have paper and a pen with you to write down any items you need to replace!

3. Do the empty shelves need a quick dusting or swipe with a damp sponge? What about the floor? Now's the time to sweep up the dust bunnies. Once that's done, you can organize and put things away.

   Doesn't it feel good to have a clean pantry? **I LOVE IT!**

GET YOUR KIDS INVOLVED!

Once everything is pulled out and expired items are thrown away, have your child organize everything and put it all back in.

The Six List: The $25,000 Piece of Advice

*Before you eat the elephant, make sure you
know what parts you want to eat.*

TODD STOCKER, *Refined: Turning Pain into Purpose*

THE LINE THROUGH MY handwritten words makes me smile.

Another thing checked off my list. *It feels good.* I love accomplishing my goals. My list for today? Just six things:

1. Spend time in the Word.
2. Put Caroline's ballet outfits out so they are ready for her practice recital.
3. Add stories to each devotional I'm working on.

4. Straighten up the house.
5. Have a breakfast plan ready for the morning (Sunday).
6. Read to my kids.

Six simple things. Oh yes, there is more to my day, and this day in particular—a Saturday—is a writing day for me. But with all the things that call to me for attention, if I can accomplish those six things, I will go to bed with a mind at rest.

Only Six Things

I used to be a Mary Kay lady. It's true—lipstick, red jacket, tights, and all! And I have to say, I'm thankful for my Mary Kay days because of one very important piece of information I was introduced to: The Six Most Important Things List.

The "Six List" originated during the 1920s when a public relations expert by the name of Ivy Lee approached Charles Schwab, the president of Bethlehem Steel, with a proposition: If Lee could have a few minutes with each executive of Schwab's company, he promised that their productivity would increase. When Schwab asked how much this secret formula was going to set him back, Lee said it would cost nothing up front. But if the strategy worked after three months, Schwab could pay Lee what he thought it was worth. Schwab agreed. When Lee met with the executives individually, he gave each person simple instructions—before leaving the office at the end of the day, make a list of the six most important things to do the next day, in order of importance, completing them as time permitted. Well, it worked. The Six List secret worked so well that Schwab wrote out a check to Lee for $25,000 (this during a time when an average worker made just under $600 a year)!

The Six List secret can work for you too!

It is so very simple.

Every night before bed write down the top six things, in order, that you need to accomplish the next day (no more than six). Then, go systematically through the list, completing the tasks in order, crossing out each thing as you go.

That's it. That's the secret.

The story goes that when Schwab sent Lee the check, he also included a note saying the advice was the most profitable business lesson he had ever learned. I bet it is just as profitable in other ways for us homemakers. Want to give it a try?

Mary Challenge

 READ PROVERBS 24:27 ·····························

Before you make your Six List, consider what needs your attention first. How are your children's hearts? What do they need from you before you begin the tasks of the day?

_____

_____

_____

_____

_____

_____

_____

_____

_____

_____

_____

_____

_____

_____

Print out the Six List found at sarahmae.com/marthamary. Use it for six days in a row. Put the most important things first, and then finish them in order (do not skip around). What you don't accomplish on that day's list, put at the top of the next day's list.

_____

_____

_____

_____

_____

_____

_____

_____

_____

Be sure to tweet me at @sarahmae or comment on my Facebook page at Facebook.com/sarahmaewrites to let me know how it goes!

MARTHA CHALLENGE

LET'S MOVE ON TO THE BATHROOMS, SHALL WE?

I know some of us have only one bathroom and some of us have five. We are going to take them one at a time, but we are only going through two in this book since I believe that is what the average house has.

If you have more than two, I'm going to assume you also have a maid, so this shouldn't be too hard for you. (I'm kidding, I'm kidding!) No matter how many bathrooms you have, let's do this!

 HERE IS YOUR GAME PLAN FOR BATHROOM #1: _____

1. Get a bin of some sort and put everything from the surface areas of your bathroom into it. Take the bin out of the bathroom. Take out the trash can as well.

2. Pour toilet bowl cleaner in the bowl and let it sit.

3. Wash the mirror, the sink, and then the toilet. Flush!

4. Wash out the bathtub.

5. Sweep the floor.

6. Get a bucket of hot, soapy water and wash the floor. If you want to get it really clean (especially around the toilet and ESPECIALLY if you have boys), get on your hands and knees to do this.

7. Put everything back in the bathroom that you want in the bathroom. (Don't put the dirty clothes back on the floor!)

Don't forget to take out the trash.

GET YOUR KIDS INVOLVED!

Trust me, your kids are capable of more than they sometimes let on. I know for sure that any kiddo seven years old and up can help clean a bathroom, even if it's just one of the steps listed.

If you have an older child who can handle the entire thing, suggest that it be his or her weekly job.

If you have younger children, assign them a part of the bathroom to clean, such as sweeping the floor and putting a new trash bag in the trash can.

DAY 6

Overcoming the Curse

Then to Adam He said, "Because you have listened to the voice of your wife, and have eaten from the tree about which I commanded you, saying, 'You shall not eat from it'; cursed is the ground because of you; in toil you will eat of it all the days of your life. Both thorns and thistles it shall grow for you; and you will eat the plants of the field."

GENESIS 3:17-18

I'M TIRED.

I know I should clean the kitchen because there is an unpleasant smell coming from there that is starting to make me feel ill. Maybe milk at the bottom of a cereal bowl that was left out? Why does milk have to smell so bad when it goes sour?

Why does milk even go sour? And why is my body so tired? I got enough sleep last night. I think I'm eating somewhat healthily. If I only had more energy, my house would be clean.

And then there's dust.

I think dust is part of the Curse.

I know that weeds are part of it because "cursed is the ground," but what about our homes? Are we fighting aspects of the Curse there, too? We battle our sin nature, which includes laziness and selfishness, but could the Fall also have to do with the fact that we just get so tired that our bodies break down and we ache, and we don't have boundless energy?

Yes, I'm convinced that dust and our clothes wearing out and things breaking down are all part of the Curse.

When sin entered the world, God pronounced judgment on the world and us, causing our domains to rebel against us just as we have rebelled against God. Our commands to rule, subdue, and be productive are all the harder to fulfill. I don't understand what it all means and exactly how it all plays out, but I do know there is toil involved.

Characteristics of the Curse

"All of creation now tends toward death, decay, and disorder. Work is not the curse; *unproductive* work is the curse (destroys your labor). Pollution pictures sin. Evil is temporary and abnormal."[1]

So how do we overcome this? How do we use the Curse to motivate us?

Here's how:

We have to keep our eyes on the eternal value of our work. If we are in Christ, then everything we do not only has value here on earth, but also has value for eternity. We have work that was created by God for us to do, and we have the power, approval, and authority to carry it out. We also have to remember the Lord is using our domains and the struggles that come with them to perfect us in our worship and service to Him.

> *Consider it all joy, my brethren, when you encounter various trials, knowing that the testing of your faith produces endurance. And let endurance have its perfect result, so that you may be perfect and complete, lacking in nothing.* JAMES 1:2-4

How we take care of our homes is all about our response to God. He gave us our homes. We have the ability to give life to them. We have to decide what our response to Him will be. Will we respond grudgingly and feel hopeless because it's just another rule to follow, or will we accept our tasks with joy, giving thanks for all the goodness and blessings we have been given? Remember, He knows our weaknesses, and He's not looking for perfection. (He already sees us as saints if we are covered with the blood of Jesus.)

Taking care of our homes is a responsibility to take joy and honor in, and ultimately is a service that will lead us toward Christlike character and humility.

Mary Challenge

 READ ROMANS 8:20-21 ·····························

What is the hope in the Curse?

_____

_____

_____

_____

_____

Think back to a time when God refined your character through difficult circumstances. Write it down and thank Him for His faithfulness.

_____

_____

_____

_____

_____

_____

_____

MARTHA CHALLENGE

IT'S TIME TO CLEAN OUT THE BATHROOM CLOSETS OR NOOKS IN YOUR FIRST BATHROOM.

 HERE IS THE PLAN: _____

1. Pull everything out of the closet onto the floor or take it to a space where you can go through everything easily.

2. Get a trash bag and a box (or something else to hold donations).

3. Sort each item into one of three categories: trash (hello, trash bag), keep, or donate. (Yes, you might have something that is nearly new that you really don't use or need.)

4. Take the donation box IMMEDIATELY to your car and either drop the stuff off after you finish or do it another day this week.

5. Once you have sorted everything, organize the items that are left and put them back into the closet.

6. *Voilà!* You are done for the day!

GET YOUR KIDS INVOLVED!

Who says you have to organize all by yourself? Get your kiddos to help. If you have a child who is willing to organize, let go of the control and let your young helper put everything away—just give your child some simple guidelines. Help is help and it is welcome!

DAY 7

Your Cleaning Style

*O Lord, You have searched me and known me. You . . . are
intimately acquainted with all my ways. . . . For You formed
my inward parts; You wove me in my mother's womb.*

PSALM 139:1-3, 13

THE KIDS ARE OUT with my husband. I had asked him if
I could have the house to myself for a little while to get my
head clear and get a few things done. He obliged. Love that
man.

I put on my favorite relaxing Pandora station, make some
tea, light a candle, bring the laundry up from the laundry
room, and begin to fold it slowly.

Listening to music and folding clothes is soothing to me.
I like working slowly and rhythmically, enjoying the process,
not rushing. I feel a sense of peace, a wonderful calm, and
even *delight*.

My sister, on the other hand, is a cleaning firecracker. When she folds laundry or cleans the kitchen or does any other housework, it's fast and efficient. She works hard and quick, and to her credit, her home is almost always clean. This "just get it done" spirit is her style. It's great because it works for her.

And my style—my slow and melodic way—is great, too, *because it works for me.*

We all operate in different ways, and I don't think one is better than the other. I do think we need to identify our style and go with it, because taking tips from others is helpful and good, but trying to *be* like others is damaging and demeaning. I have accepted that I am never going to be like Martha Stewart. That's okay.

God formed our personalities, and He knows how we work and how we don't. He knows where we struggle and where we excel. If you are not a naturally neat and organized type A personality, just accept it, and live out who you are. I used to beat myself up all the time thinking, *If only I were like so-and-so, I would be such a better wife, homemaker, mother.* We do have a responsibility to our families and the homes God gave us, but let's not get trapped by perfection, comparisons, or any other distractions that steal away the truth that God loves us and we are works in progress!

I want you to think about your personality style and what works for you.

Maybe you love the idea of having a schedule and you

are great at writing one out, but when it comes to actually following it, well, let's just say, not so much! Perhaps for the time being, you need to not be scheduled, but instead focus on getting certain tasks accomplished by a certain time in the day. For example, set a goal to have your kitchen clean after breakfast. However, maybe for you, mornings are better spent hanging out with your kiddos and just gathering yourself for the day. So you might say, "I will have my kitchen cleaned by noon." That's a realistic goal that doesn't put you in a box; there is freedom in flexibility. And maybe you don't want a schedule at all, but would like some anchors in your days to create consistency. For example, you might set specific times for breakfast, reading, laundry, and dinner.

No matter what plan you choose, remember this: *Don't beat yourself up!* I don't care how many times you fail, don't quit; press on, and know who you are in Jesus. Figure out your cleaning style and go with it, not trying to be anybody else. Work hard, get done what you need to, confess laziness, and accept God's grace. Oh, and know you are not alone— I'm here encouraging you!

Mary Challenge

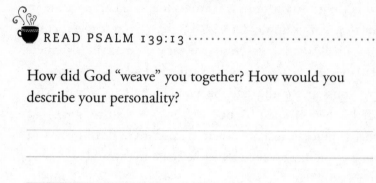

READ PSALM 139:13 ·······························

How did God "weave" you together? How would you describe your personality?

_____

_____

_____

_____

_____

_____

Just for fun take the DISC personality test (http://
www.quibblo.com/quiz/aw8npyx/DISC-Personality-Style)
and get to know *yourself* better. You will find more about
the DISC test, including descriptions of the different
personality styles, at http://www.discinsights.com/cyber
/scripts/disc.asp.

MARTHA CHALLENGE

TODAY, MY FRIENDS, WE MOVE INTO THE
LIVING ROOM.

 PICK UP _____

1. Begin by picking up anything that doesn't belong in the living room and get it out of there. If the items belong to the kids, ask them to put these things away. Make sure nothing is on the floor that shouldn't be on the floor.

2. Fluff up and put your pillows or throw blankets on your chairs and couches. Isn't that pretty?

 WORK ON ONE AREA AT A TIME _____

3. Perhaps you have a mantel or a piano or a space for toys. Pick one of those areas and remove everything from the surface and dust, sort items, rearrange, and organize. Be sure to clean and organize one area at a time; when you have completed an area, you can move on to the next one.

4. Do everything in the living room except the bookshelves (if they are located in the living room) and the floor (if you have wood floors). We'll begin those chores tomorrow.

DAY 8

Making Your Personality Work for You

*My frame was not hidden from You, when I was made in
secret, and skillfully wrought in the depths of the earth.*

PSALM 139:15

WE TURN THE MUSIC up loud.

My youngest daughter and I begin to dance, moving all
around the living room. I pick her up and swing her around,
and she giggles and I love it. I twist and shake and throw
some pillows on the couch.

"Care, dance yourself over to your Barbies on the floor
and take them to your room, please."

She shimmies over and starts to pick them up.

My son can't *not* dance. He has the beat in his bones

and does his own little jig, which always makes me laugh. He has such zeal. I ask him to pick up his Legos and put them away.

"Mom! Turn the music down!" my oldest daughter shouts. She doesn't want to dance; she's listening to an audiobook while cleaning her room. Dancing is not her thing when it comes to cleaning. That's okay, I'll get her to dance later. She'll resist, and then she'll break into a smile, and after we've twirled around the room numerous times, we'll eventually fall on the couch out of breath.

We dance, we clean, we listen, we giggle, we get frustrated, we yell, we work, and we eventually get it done.

This is how we do it.

I hope that you took the DISC test I mentioned so you have discovered your personality style.

I believe this information about personalities is super helpful, but I don't think we need to rely solely on it or become obsessed with it. Still, it can help us better understand our strengths and weaknesses, and how we can use them in our cleaning and organization efforts.

Today we're going to look at the best ways to get and stay motivated for each personality style. Here we go!

The "D" Style

You are very results oriented and you like the bottom line. You look for the fastest way possible to get your work done. You thrive on challenges, and you are also a great motivator. Let's use these qualities to get you moving!

MOTIVATION: CHALLENGE

You need to be challenged, so try giving yourself a challenge each day. Maybe it's one big challenge or a few small ones. Either way, you will achieve real results if you meet your challenges. If, for example, you want to go to sleep in a clean bedroom each night, challenge yourself to spend twenty minutes a day straightening up your room and making your bed. Challenge yourself to do it during a particular time of the day until it becomes a habit, say between 9:00 and 9:20 every morning. You need to see results or you will soon give up, so developing a habit for yourself is imperative! Go on. Challenge yourself to form one new habit and give it all you've got!

The "I" Style

You would rather do practically anything than clean. You're superfun and very people oriented, so cleaning your home with no one to really talk to but little ones is extrahard on you. If only you could have someone over every day to talk and clean with you, this whole cleaning thing wouldn't be so bad!

MOTIVATION: POSITIVE FEEDBACK/FUN

Here are some ways you can get motivated:

1. Reward yourself or have someone reward you for doing certain tasks. Work something out with your hubby or your mother or your sister or a friend. For example, if you keep your home in order and clean for a week, your husband takes you out to dinner or

some other thing you enjoy. Set tangible goals that you have to meet, but keep them small and realistic. You are not detail oriented!

2. Have fun with cleaning! Play your music loud, dance while you clean—whatever you do, just make it fun!

3. You dream of having a clean home, but you just don't think it's possible with your personality. It is! You can and will have a clean and welcoming home! Just think—if you can keep your home tidy, you will be more willing to have people over and be the fun hostess that you are!

4. Ask your husband/loved ones/friends/kids to tell you when you are doing a good job—you need all the encouragement you can get. Negative feedback just puts you in a slump!

The "S" Style

You are a sweetie! S types are friendly and steady—you make us D types melt! You are extremely loyal and supportive; you need security and stability. If someone is willing to gently guide you and teach you ways to be clean and organized, you will fare well under your teacher's authority. In fact, you enjoy having someone guide you. You find comfort in it.

MOTIVATION: AFFIRMATION

You need to be affirmed by being told that what you're doing matters, and that you're doing a good job. Here are some tips that might help you:

1. Ask your husband or kids to affirm you when you do a good job.
2. Affirm yourself! This may be difficult for you, but when you complete a goal or give your best effort, tell yourself, "Good job!" Thank God that He is the ultimate provider of stability and security, and His promises will never fail.
3. Find a program that teaches and guides you.

The "C" Style

You are a superdetailed person, and you love structure and quality. You are a natural organizer, but you can sometimes be critical and a perfectionist, which can get in the way of the big picture. You seek facts, and you want to know the most systematic way to get things done. Quite frankly, you probably don't even need this book!

MOTIVATION: STRUCTURE

Make a schedule and get yourself into a routine. (Seriously, like I need to even tell you this!) You won't have much trouble with consistency, but what you may have trouble with is how to do everything "right" and still relax to spend time with your husband or kiddos. You need to have realistic expectations to get what you need done, but without expecting perfection. Strive for excellence, but land in the softness of grace.

{ Mary Challenge }

READ PSALM 119:73 ·

Why can we rely on God for understanding?

_____

_____

_____

_____

_____

What does He give us that helps us understand His character?

_____

_____

_____

_____

Try one of the ideas listed under the motivation for your personality style.

MARTHA CHALLENGE

TODAY YOU ARE GOING TO CLEAN AND ORGANIZE YOUR BOOKSHELVES.

You will want to set aside at least an hour or two for this job, especially if you get distracted when you start looking through your books!

HERE'S THE PLAN: _____

1. Get a big box or trash bag for books you are going to give away.

2. Take all the books off your shelf and begin to sort them, putting giveaway books directly into the box or bag.

3. Dust your shelves.

4. Place the books back on the shelves.

    Doesn't it look wonderful? Give yourself a pat on the back. You're done for today! Tomorrow, floors!

DAY 9

Tornado Cleaning

Git-R-Done!

LARRY THE CABLE GUY

MY SISTER KEITHA IS an inspiration to me.

She came to visit me on Wednesday and by Saturday the house was a wreck. We'd been too busy talking, making my brother watch *Jurassic Park* (he was twenty-three and he'd never seen it!), and driving all over town doing fun things together. I wanted to get my home in order before Sunday so my family could relax. I also knew that I'd put off the cleaning until the last possible minute.

Now it was Saturday evening. I decided to get the babes a movie so I could just focus on cleaning. When I got home from Redbox, I walked into a tornado—a cleaning tornado.

Now mind you, I am like a butterfly. I flit around from thing to thing, getting something done here and then there, getting caught up in distraction and flowing along with the breeze. I take my time when I clean; in other words, I'm slow. Really slow. (My sister couldn't believe it took me forty-five minutes to clean my girls' bedroom. Sorry, Sis.)

Remember, I like to listen to music, and as I'm cleaning I look through the things I'm dusting or rearranging, ponder on something for a bit, remember that I have to answer an e-mail, think about that shirt I want to wash, and oh yeah, I need to get a new whatsit the next time I'm out. Wouldn't the pillows be prettier if I arranged them like this? Yes, much better. Okay, now where was I? The dishes, right . . .

Writing this is kind of how I clean. I'm already distracted and need to get back to the story at hand. Where was I?

Ah yes, my sister, the tornado.

So I come home, walk into the kitchen, and see that it's clean. (Let's just pause here and say a little "hallelujah" because I didn't have to clean it.)

She's in there whipping those pans into shape. "Wow, you're fast," I say. "I've only been gone for ten minutes." She clears the dining room table, scrubs it clean, picks up trash, and tells my kids what they need to do to help—no movie until the house is clean. I'm just standing there, watching, and she says, "If you just work fast and get it done, then you'll have time to do the things you want to do."

Just like that, matter of fact.

Just do it. And do it *fast.*

Before I knew it, I was running around cleaning, and so were my children! We all became cleaning tornadoes and within fifteen minutes, the upstairs main spaces were clean.

How to Be a Cleaning Tornado
GIVE YOURSELF A CHALLENGE AND DO IT IN A SET AMOUNT OF TIME

There is something about a challenge and a time limit that makes you focus and move. It is incredibly effective to go into cleaning mode and just do the work as fast as you can. One of the inspirations I have is from the 31 Days to Clean: Mamas of Little Ones Facebook group. They give each other challenges that have to be done within a set time frame. They hustle and do whatever they can in that ten or fifteen minutes' span of time, and then they encourage one another and do virtual high fives before moving on with their days. Which brings me to this . . .

DON'T CLEAN ALONE

The women in the Mamas of Little Ones Facebook group live all over the United States and yet they clean together and encourage each other daily. They've been doing this for about a year now. These women have not only come up with a system (Task #1, 2, 3, 4), but they jump on when they have the time and just ask, "Anyone up for a challenge?" Within a few minutes someone else jumps on and they pick a task and go for it together, even though they are miles apart. I love it. Here are some of the quotes I've seen in the group:

> "I am SO THANKFUL to have ladies to work with today! I need encouragement and motivation!"

> "Okay lovely ladies! On to #1!!! WE can do this!!!"

> "BREAK!! What did you get done so far?"

> - "I got started on the kitchen and took a phone call from my doctor . . . Second half will be stronger!"

> - "I got all the dirty laundry moved to the laundry room, sorted, and a load started, and I exercised for ten minutes!"

GET HYPERFOCUSED

If I have to clean fast, I've got to get focused. No music, no organizing, no e-mails, no nothing. Just hone in on the task at hand and go, go, go! I've seen my sister do this, and it works wonders! Once I finish the task at hand, then I can listen to my music and slow clean or organize something else that isn't a priority.

GET THE BABES INVOLVED

It's amazing what a child can do when there is a clear focus about attaining a goal together quickly. I couldn't believe everything that my children finished with my no-nonsense sister directing them. They had no option but to clean, and so clean they did! I admit that I am not as firm with making the children help me. I either move too slow myself, which doesn't motivate them, or I get upset that they are not cleaning fast enough. (They get distracted so easily; hmmm . . . I wonder where that comes from?)

Watching my sister helped me realize I just need to say, "Okay, loves, we're a family, a team, and we're going to get this done in this amount of time and then we can play." I find that when I give my children specific age-appropriate tasks, they do the work. It also helps if they know they have a reward when they're done: They can play, go outside, watch a movie, get a treat, or something else.

Mary Challenge

READ PROVERBS 31:17-21 ·

What are some of the benefits the Proverbs 31 woman received from working hard and "gitting-r-done"?

_____

_____

_____

_____

What are some of the benefits you have found when you git-r-done?

_____

_____

_____

_____

Do you have a friend, a sister, a mother, or a mentor whom you admire for the personable touch she has created in her home? Ask her for some advice and/or tips on how she does it.

 MARTHA CHALLENGE

SWEEP, VACUUM, AND/OR WASH YOUR LIVING ROOM FLOOR.

⏱ 15 MINUTE CHALLENGE _____

Just for fun (wink wink), give yourself a fifteen-minute challenge. Pick something that needs to be done in your house, perhaps just cleaning a main space, and set your timer for fifteen minutes. Get hyperfocused and get as much done in that time frame as you can. See if you can recruit your babes to help as well!

Slow and Steady

Life is not an emergency.

ANN VOSKAMP

IF I LET MY house go for a few days, it becomes overwhelming to clean. I look around at the piles and the papers, and I purpose in my heart that I am going to become a minimalist and just throw everything away.

When I'm feeling overwhelmed with my house and my to-do list, and tornado cleaning just isn't what I'm in the mood for, I think, *Slow and steady. One step at a time.* My friend Amy taught me that, and I'm learning . . . slow and steady. Pick that up. Put it away. Wash that dish, sweep, put on some music, fold clothes, do a little dance with my kids, *keep on.* Slow and steady.

And when my heart hurts and the waves of discouragement come full on, I have to slow and steady myself. Slow, *seek Him in the still place.* Steady, *lean on the firm One.* Some days, slow and steady is the only way I make it through.

Whatever it is today that seems chaotic—your home, your seemingly out-of-control child, your work, your marriage, your soul—think, *slow and steady.*

One step at a time, one day at a time, slow and steady, *you'll make it.*

Mary Challenge

 READ MATTHEW 6:25-33 ....

Think about something in your life that you need to stop striving frantically to put in order. Is there truly any need to rush? What are some gifts that come from slowing down and taking a steady approach to things?

_____

_____

_____

_____

_____

_____

_____

_____

Is there a place in your home or your soul where you need stillness? Whisper these phrases as you breathe in and out, "Slow and steady. One step at a time." You've got this. And He's got you.

MARTHA CHALLENGE

CATCH-UP DAY!

 **CONTINUE WORKING**

Whatever you didn't finish yesterday, continue working on it today—slow and steady.

Commit your way to the LORD,
Trust also in Him, and He will do it.

PSALM 37:5

DAY 11

A Place to Put Your Feet Up

Frodo was now safe in the Last Homely House east of the Sea.
That house was, as Bilbo had long ago reported, "a perfect house,
whether you like food or sleep or story-telling or singing, or just
sitting and thinking best, or a pleasant mixture of them all."
Merely to be there was a cure for weariness, fear, and sadness.

J. R. R. TOLKIEN, *The Fellowship of the Ring*

I'M JUST ABOUT AT Amy's house.

I pull up and I barely get parked when my kids jump out to greet her kids. They all head straight for the trampoline. *See you in a couple of hours,* I think to myself, smiling.

I head in and Amy has coffee made and some sort of snack. My favorite is the homemade gingersnaps she made over the Christmas holiday. *To die for.* Today, she has banana bread. We chat in the kitchen as she sweeps up some crumbs that she'll be sweeping up again before I leave. Five kids. There is always something to sweep up.

We get our coffee and our bread and settle ourselves on the off-white couch for some good conversation. Toys are on the floor, but that's okay because the place feels happy. I notice a chocolate bar on the end table. Amy gives me a wink and says, "For later."

I love it here.

Have you ever walked into someone's home and felt like you couldn't get comfortable? The whole place was just too clean, too put-together, too . . . untouchable?

There is something to be said for a space that invites rest, a "come-on-in-and-prop-your-feet-up" kind of beckoning. I like places like that. I like melting into a comfy couch that was made for long hours of coffee and conversation.

Cleaning isn't just about scrubbing floors, making beds, and clearing out clutter—although those are good things. It's also about creating an environment that encourages people to feel welcomed and loved. I believe one of the ways we can give love through our homes is to have a "put your feet up" atmosphere. Here are some ideas to do just that.

5 Ways to Create a Sense of "Welcome! Put Your Feet Up"

1. Don't, under any circumstances, have plastic coverings on your furniture. Nothing says *uncomfortable* like plastic under your behind.

2. Do consider having some throw blankets and soft decorative pillows around that whisper, "Go ahead and get comfy, friend; you won't wear out your welcome."

3. Don't make everything perfect. Let your home be lived in and let others experience that lived-in feel.

4. Always have coffee or tea made (or ready to be made).

5. Be a listener.

The goal of homemaking isn't to have perfectly decorated, perfectly clean homes. The whole point is to have a place that is welcoming, and you know where that begins? In your own heart.

Your home is a reflection of who you are. If you are warm and welcoming, your home will be. The cleaning? That's just the cherry on top, you know, so no one trips on the way to your couch.

Here's to putting our feet up and staying awhile!

Mary Challenge

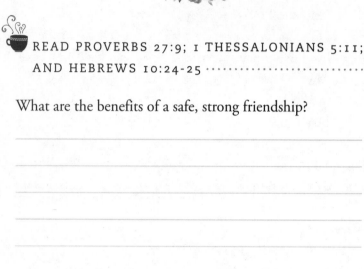

READ PROVERBS 27:9; I THESSALONIANS 5:11;
AND HEBREWS 10:24-25 ·····························

What are the benefits of a safe, strong friendship?

_____

_____

_____

_____

_____

_____

_____

_____

Invite a friend over and encourage her to put her feet up.
Don't worry about making everything just right! Brew
some coffee, get a snack, and enjoy good conversation. In
fact, I double challenge you: Listen well and make your
guest feel loved and special.

MARTHA CHALLENGE

TODAY ON THE DOCKET WE BEGIN BEDROOMS!

This is another one of those challenges that may need to be adjusted depending on how many bedrooms you have in your home.

We have four bedrooms in our home, three for the babes and one for my husband and me.

We are going to split bedrooms into seven days of cleanup, which includes closets. If you need more time than that, plan accordingly—perhaps a weekend cleaning day. If you need less time, use the days off to bake. Or—my preference—spend them reading a good book!

HERE'S WHAT WE'RE GOING TO DO _____

1. Tackle the oldest child's bedroom first, enlisting his or her help or having that child do it if he or she is old enough.

2. Put all the dirty clothes into a laundry basket and all the clean clothes (why are there clean clothes on the floor?) on the bed.

3. Put all toys and books and miscellaneous things on the bed. (Yes, it's crowded, but it works.)

4. Pick up all the trash and throw it out! You should now have nothing on the floor.

5. Pull things off any unordered, disheveled shelves and off the top of dressers.

6. Clean the shelves and surfaces.

7. Put the clean clothes away.

8. Put the books away.

9. Put the toys or other things away.

10. If you or your child has a desk, go ahead and get that cleaned out and cleaned up. If your child has a messy desk, he or she is probably old enough to clean it alone.

11. Vacuum or sweep the floor.

Do not wash the bedding yet because I don't want you to get burned out. We'll save the bedding for another day.

DAY 12

Feeling Overwhelmed

Don't worry about anything; instead, pray about everything. Tell God what you need, and thank him for all he has done. Then you will experience God's peace, which exceeds anything we can understand. His peace will guard your hearts and minds as you live in Christ Jesus.

PHILIPPIANS 4:6-7, NLT

THE HOUSE IS A mess—*again*. Dishes all over the counter-tops, toys everywhere, papers askew, laundry piled up, and overall "I'm-so-behind-on-life" disarray. It's depressing just looking at it all. *Didn't I just get this mess cleaned up?*

When I look around at the mess, I see Mount Everest. I get stuck, I feel depressed, and I have no idea where to begin or if I even want to. I just feel so overwhelmed sometimes.

After learning about the Curse, I at least have a clearer perspective on my housework. I can see the eternal reasons for taking care of my home and family, and the immediate gratification of a well-kept home is like the frosting on the cake. But I still struggle with being overwhelmed from time to time. So, what's a girl to do?

Here are some tips I've come across over the years, suggestions that have been helpful to me:

- *When the house is a mess, work on only one room at a time.* This little nugget of advice has helped me so much! I tend to just start cleaning, haphazardly moving from room to room, cleaning a little here and a little there. Then I started doing only one room at a time—what a difference! I stay focused on my task, and when I'm through with one room, I can look at it and see results.
- *Be generous to your trash can.* Throw things out! The more things I realize I don't need and can definitely live without, the less stress I create for myself. Just let it go!
- *Get rid of half the toys.* I'm serious. Okay fine, maybe for you half is too much (or not enough), but the point is, your kiddos don't need to have five thousand things. Grab the toys the kiddos don't play with all that much (or won't even notice that they're gone) and either get rid of them or store them in the attic. You can always pull them out on a rainy day.
- *Do the fifteen-minute thing.* Professional organizer Marla Cilley (aka the FlyLady)[1] suggests putting the timer on for fifteen minutes and going to work, doing everything you can in that amount of time. Imposing a time constraint is helpful, especially to those of us who like a challenge. Turn on some Pandora radio, and you're set!

- *Just get moving!* I spend so much time fretting and feeling overwhelmed that I stay stagnant, which leads me to feeling worse, and then ultimately, I give in to laziness and a "why bother?" attitude. Just get up! Force yourself to do *something* because as it's been said, "Action is the antidote to despair."

- *Envision the big picture.* You know that warm and comfy feeling you get when you walk into a home that is well cared for, clean, and inviting? It's not sterile (i.e., no plastic coverings on the furniture), but tidy, warm, and peaceful. That's the kind of home I want, and that motivates me to see the big picture instead of the piles. What's your big picture?

- *Get off the computer.* This is probably the best advice I can give you. For me, the more I'm on the computer, the more depressed I get and the less I do. Shut it down, friend.

- *Keep your eyes on the goal.* I believe getting our work done while pushing through the tough stuff will reap eternal rewards. Your family (and even you) will be more comfortable and less stressed. Think on these outcomes as you persevere up the mountain. The view from the top will be exhilarating or, at the very least, peaceful and clean.

- *Get something new for your home that brings a smile to your face.* Buy or find something to put in your home that matches the vision you have for your space. Perhaps it will be something unique you nab at a yard sale this weekend, something you repurpose, or something beautiful that lifts your spirit. Whatever it is, find it, place it, and enjoy it.

Mary Challenge

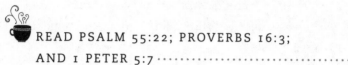

READ PSALM 55:22; PROVERBS 16:3;
AND 1 PETER 5:7 ·····································

When we are feeling overwhelmed, what does Jesus ask us
to do?

_____

_____

_____

_____

Light a candle, find a cozy spot somewhere quiet (only for
ten minutes—send the kids outside, wait until nap time, or
pop in a DVD), sip on your favorite beverage, close your eyes,
and envision your big picture. Think about your home and
what you want it to be. Do you want it to be a place of refuge?
Inviting? Warm? Fun? Picture your home in all its clean and
organized glory, and then burn the image into your heart and
mind. Now grab a pen and write down your big picture on
the lines provided (or in your journal, a separate notebook, or
on a piece of paper). Ask God to help you physically create the
vision for your home life.

Ask yourself what your stressors are. Can your children or husband help relieve some of that stress? For example, I taught my eight-year-old how to do laundry so she could be responsible for her clothes.

MARTHA CHALLENGE

TODAY, FOCUS ON YOUR BEDROOM CLOSET.

 Get rid of everything you don't use or haven't used in two years. Let it go, friend, just let it go.

MOTHER-IN-LAW'S NOTE

If you don't want to just get rid of everything you haven't used in two years, play mix and match with your clothes and see if you can create outfits using some of the things you haven't worn. Sometimes I see a bunch of clothes I haven't worn, discard them, and then later regret getting rid of them. If you make interchangeable outfits, you can pare down your closet that way.

 READERS' TIPS

I take everything off the floor of the closet and then vacuum that space. I put last season's shoes in a storage bin and take it to the garage. Same thing with last season's clothes. I pitch all metal and plastic hangers, using only wooden ones. They last longer and look prettier in my opinion. Then I clear off the top shelves, dust off the shelving, and organize books, purses, photos, and random items by putting them in small storage boxes with labels. I also take this time to change out the lightbulbs. Then I Febreze the closet and *voilà!*[2]

–Melinda Stanley

In the bathroom closet, instead of folding my towels, I roll them. They take up less space and look nicer that way.[3]

–Kristine Huber

Purge, Baby, Purge

Does this spark joy?

MARIE KONDO,
THE LIFE-CHANGING MAGIC OF TIDYING UP

LATELY I HAVE BEEN obsessed with purging.

I love getting rid of things. In fact, I think I'm a minimalist at heart; it just hasn't played out in my reality yet. This is mainly because I haven't made the time to get rid of things; I've always thought I just needed to sort and organize. But then I read Marie Kondo's wonderful little book, *The Life-Changing Magic of Tidying Up*.[1] While Marie and I don't track philosophically, she did help me see two things that have been a tremendous help in getting clarity with my cleaning.

First, she says when you keep organizing things that you don't really need, you are just keeping a mess. I would suspect that you're like me. We reorganize papers and mementos and clothes and all sorts of things, but we never really rid ourselves of what doesn't bring us joy.

Which brings me to the second and most helpful thing: *Keep only that which brings you joy.*[2] What a game changer for me! To keep only what speaks to my heart and sparks joy is such a beautiful way to live. I will admit that I have extended the idea to also keeping what I believe will bring my children joy and teach them. So we keep educational resources as well.

I first experienced the freedom of purging when I went through my bookshelves. Yes, bookshelves. I know, I know—never get rid of books; they are like babies or best friends. I hear you! But hear *me*. When I cleaned off my shelves and got rid of the books that were just taking up space, I felt lighter and happier because I knew that the only books that were on my shelves were those that bring me *joy*.

After that first experience of downsizing my library, I have become a junkie. Here are the reasons I'm going to keep purging other areas of my home:

CLEAR SPACE, CLEAR MIND

There is something so liberating for both the mind and spirit when your house is free of stuff. I don't just feel lighter; I can think more clearly, and it seems as though there is more "white space" in my soul. I don't like tripping over items scattered on the floor in my home, and I don't like tripping over tugging thoughts that get in the way of important ones. Believe me, when you have a clear space, you will find you have a clearer mind as well.

LESS TO CLEAN
I mean, who doesn't want less to clean?! Less stuff, less mess, LESS CLEANING. Can I get an amen?

BE SURROUNDED BY WHAT BRINGS YOU JOY
What a lovely concept—being around the things that bring you joy. I love it. And thanks to Marie Kondo, this is my new perspective on stuff. If it doesn't bring me or my family joy, *good-bye.*

READ MATTHEW 6:19-20 ································

What "stuff" should we focus on storing up? Why?

_____

_____

_____

_____

Look around your home. What brings you chaos? What brings you joy? What do you need to do to increase the "joy" spaces and eliminate or lessen the "chaos" spaces?

_____

_____

_____

_____

_____

_____

_____

MARTHA CHALLENGE

NATIONAL GOODWILL DAY!

In an effort to reduce accumulated stuff, I am creating National Goodwill Day! Take a look at the things you have and evaluate if you really need all that stuff. Are there things you can get rid of?

 PURGE _____

1. Go through your drawers, closets, and any other random spaces where your clothes/shoes/purses hide out and pull out anything that you realistically do not use and will not use, even those things you've saved for that one day you just know will come when you'll need that particular white purse with the silver chain. (Sorry, I digress.) And if you're saving those too-tight jeans for the day "when I'll wear them again," just give them up, my friend. In the event that you do lose that last ten pounds, celebrate by buying a new pair. Oh, those cute little trinkets from Aunt Mary—gone! Purge, baby, purge! For some of you, this will be very hard, like letting go of some good friends, but sometimes, you've just got to let go.

2. Remember, you're not in this alone. We're here for you, we support you, and we really can't wait to pick up your once-dear "friends" on a sale rack next week for a dollar. (Thanks in advance.)

The reduction of clutter? **BLISS.**

DAY 14

The Toy Situation

If you want your children to turn out well, spend twice as
much time with them and half as much money.

ABIGAIL VAN BUREN

THERE HE WAS, SITTING on his bed with tears in his
seven-year-old eyes.

I had just yelled at him again to clean his bedroom. I was
tired of the mess, and I was tired of telling him to clean.

"Just do it!" I shouted. How quickly I forget how overwhelmed I feel when a mess is staring me in the face.

This was not the mother I wanted to be.

As I looked at my son and I looked at the mess, I realized
we were both overwhelmed. It was too much; it felt like too
high a mountain to climb.

It was then that I knew we needed a change. My sweet

boy needed a mom who wasn't so stressed, and I needed a boy who didn't feel defeated before he began.

That was the day we decided on a very simple rule that would become the foundation for how we would live: fewer things, more peace.

The less we have, the less overwhelmed we feel. And the less overwhelmed we feel, the happier we are.

It was with that philosophy in mind that I said, "Buddy, we are going to get rid of some things today. We can throw some things away and give some things away, but at the end of it all, you are only going to have twenty toys left."

We called it "The Twenty-Toy Rule."

Twenty toys sounds like a lot . . . or maybe it doesn't. I admit that I was shocked when I saw how many things my kiddos had accumulated. My husband and I make an effort not to spoil our children, and I already had been pretty strict about the number of toys per child. But when I sat with my son in his room that day, I had to face the fact that we had allowed too much stuff.

When I proposed my idea to him, my son's eyes got big at first and he looked worried. But once we started, he really got into it. He was sorting and getting excited about giving things away and even selling things in a future yard sale. He was, believe it or not, actually having fun with the challenge.

The more we got rid of, the lighter I felt. And the anger began to disappear. There we were, getting rid of stuff, and we were happier.

Here's the lesson for all of us. We don't need stuff, we

need peace. We need to feel loved and safe and okay with what we have.

I want my children to learn contentment and joy where they are and with what they have. I don't want them falling into the trap of always needing more and better things. Learning to have less helps them to be free. And I want them to be free.

To be fair, keeping toys to a minimum has taken work. I have had to train my three children to be okay with not having something else. And yes, it has been training. For example, every time we would go into Target, the first section we would come to was the dollar section filled with bright and beckoning things that call to children (thanks for that, Target). I used to think, *What's a dollar? It's no big deal.* So nearly every time we entered the store my kids would each get something. I decided that would be one of the changes I made right away—no more dollar toys. I told my children before we even went into the store what to expect, and they all nodded their little heads in understanding.

You can imagine the shock when I actually followed through. "But Mom!" No buts, baby. We are doing this. We are learning to be content. After a few times of whining and crying and me not giving in, they stopped fussing. Now we go into Target and they don't even ask. They know it wouldn't make a difference anyway.

The point is, we had to put rules in place, and we had to stick to them. It's hard at first, but if you stick to it, it gets easier. I promise.

You can do it. You can help your children be free.

It's worth it.

Mary Challenge

 READ PROVERBS 22:6 ···································

What is the long-term value of teaching your child to be content with fewer things?

_____

_____

_____

_____

_____

_____

Sit down with your child and talk to him or her about contentment and joy and the freedom that comes with having fewer things.

MARTHA CHALLENGE

TODAY LET'S PURGE!

 HELPING YOUR CHILDREN LET GO OF THINGS—A QUICK GUIDE

Only use this guide if it fits your family's philosophy. Feel free to forget it altogether if it doesn't. If your child keeps a neat and orderly room most of the time, you may just want to skip this guide. Play it by ear with each child, taking his or her personality into account.

1. Let your child know that you are going to make cleaning their room a cinch.

2. Explain that the two of you will go through all of the toys and pick and choose only twenty things to keep (or whatever number you decide). You can determine what equals one toy. Remember, you are the authority. Don't go in with a wishy-washy attitude. If you decide to do this, you need to do it. That doesn't mean you're not gentle or compassionate, it just means that you know you are doing the best thing for your child and likely for your own sanity.

3. Encourage your child as you pare down the toys. Remind them that this will help them have a cleaner room and open up more space to play.

4. Help your child understand that you will not buy toys on impulse, no matter how inexpensive. If you commit to avoid buying on impulse, it keeps toys to a manageable number, and it teaches your child contentment with what he or she has. A win-win solution!

DAY 15

Kids and Cleaning

Train up a child in the way he should go, even
when he is old he will not depart from it.

PROVERBS 22:6

KIDS CAN DO MORE than we give them credit for.

As I write this book, my children are ages six, eight, and nine. They have to clean their rooms, unload the dishwasher, and help around the house. But after talking with my sister-in-law, Sarah, recently, I realized that my children can do more than the basics. Sarah's children, who are six and eight years old, take turns cleaning up the kitchen every night after dinner. The eight-year-old is responsible for loading and running the dishwasher, washing the pots and pans, and wiping down the counters on his night. The six-year-old loads and runs the dishwasher on her night. Huh. Well then, I suppose my children can do more!

With this information in hand, I decided to teach my kids to clean the whole kitchen. I started with my nine-year-old. Not only did I ask her to clean up after dinner during the week, but I gave her the ultimate challenge—cleaning up the weekend dishes. Talk about a disaster zone in the sink. I mean, there were dishes from several meals from over the weekend! I stayed with her and taught her how to do everything, from rinsing off the dishes before putting them in the dishwasher, to loading the dishwasher, running it, washing the pots and pans, wiping down the counters, and sweeping the floor. It took about forty minutes (it really was a mess!), but she did it. I was so proud of her! And here's the kicker: She was proud of herself. She looked over the kitchen with a sense of accomplishment.

The next day, the task wasn't nearly as messy. I still needed to guide her, but she did a great job. I made a chart that listed the steps to cleaning the kitchen, just in case she needed any reminders.

Before she learned to clean the kitchen, I taught her and my son how to do their own laundry. It is not only a help to me, but it helps them because if they want their clothes clean, they are capable of doing it. It also teaches them responsibility, an asset for life.

I want all my children to know how to run a household, and I'd like them to be able to do it by age ten. I know it's possible; it's just a matter of taking the time to teach and train them. It's worth it.

Wisdom from My Sister-in-Law

I believe God wants us to do our best in everything, but relationships are especially important. The two most important commands that God has given to us are stated here: "'You shall love the Lord your God with all your heart, and with all your soul, and with all your mind.' This is the great and foremost commandment. The second is like it, 'You shall love your neighbor as yourself.'"[1] Relationships with our family and our "neighbors" are to be our top priorities. There are some things in life that you will never be able to get back—a clean house isn't one of them!

Here are some tips that have worked for me:

- *I steward my time.* I must use my time wisely. For me, that means I have to stay off social media, the phone, and the Internet. There is a time for everything. This continues to be a very difficult thing for me to discipline myself in. Colossians 3:23 says, "Whatever you do, work at it with all your heart, as working for the Lord, not for human masters" (NIV).
- *I pray that God will multiply my time and efforts.* It's amazing how this small prayer changes my attitude. Psalm 37:5 says, "Commit your way to the LORD, trust also in Him, and He will do it." God truly cares about the details of our lives!
- *I prioritize my day in this order:* God, family, and tasks. When I do, everything tends to run much smoother.
- *Often I throw a quick Crock-Pot meal together in the*

morning. When I know I have a busy day of cleaning, it is a huge relief to know a meal will be ready at the end of a productive day.

- *I get the kids to help.* As much as I can, I assign a task to each child according to his or her age and ability. I work with each of them on a task the first one or two times, teaching them the how-tos of the job; once the children learn, they are required to help out when asked, needed, or scheduled. The old saying that "many hands make light work" couldn't be truer. When a job has been done well, I verbally or sometimes monetarily praise the child. If the child asks me if the job is done well, I will ask the child if he did his best and if he would be pleased with the outcome if Jesus were to see it. I don't want the effort to be for me, but for the Lord.

I believe having a clean home creates a sense of calm in the home, although keeping it clean can feel meaningless, redundant, and constant. However, if we view our work as serving others and—by doing so—loving them, it changes our heart attitudes. When we serve those in our home by taking care of it, we become more Christlike. Jesus came to earth to serve us, so we can do the same for our families.

I fail so many times. Thankfully, our God is not a condemning God, but a gracious one, who is slow to anger and abounding in loving-kindness! Ultimately, all our efforts in this life are to glorify Him.

Mary Challenge

 READ—WITH YOUR KIDS—COLOSSIANS 3:23.

What are we encouraged to do with our work? Who is it really for?

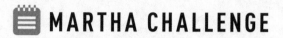 **MARTHA CHALLENGE**

TODAY, MOVE TO THE NEXT BEDROOM.
Repeat the steps from the first bedroom on Day 11.

HELP YOUR CHILDREN LEARN TO CLEAN—READERS' TIPS

Draw or write (depending on age) a list of steps for your kids' chores. Laminate the list, and stick it in the rooms where the chores need to happen. Each kid at our house has a morning routine list posted by his or her bedroom light switch, too.[2]

—Kristie Wooten

(1) Change the way you talk about chores. Explain that chores are ways that we can bless others in our household. (2) Have your children start by working alongside you, the younger ones doing what they are capable of doing. (3) Start giving all of your children responsibilities when they are young—showing them, helping them, and guiding them until they can do it themselves.[3]

—Rebecca Carter

DAY 16

I'd Rather Do Anything but Clean (When the Bones Are Feeling Lazy)

Nothing ever comes to one that is worth having,
except as a result of hard work.

BOOKER T. WASHINGTON

I LOVE TO SLEEP.

Sometimes, when I lie down in my bed at night, I just smile and wiggle my toes and think how thankful I am for sleep. It is so good.

And warm baths—love those too.

Oh, and curling up in my white comfy chair, sipping tea (sometimes coffee), and just letting my bones relax.

Relax. Curl up. Sleep. I could live like this 24-7. But it's not much of a life, and my home would fall apart and my children would essentially raise themselves, because my husband works full-time. You know, if I just lived comfortably . . . If I just let laziness have its way in me . . .

If I just chose to be selfish.

That's right, selfish. Because let's face it, the root of laziness is selfishness (which we'll talk about tomorrow). We're not talking about being genuinely tired—that's legit. We're talking about just not wanting to do anything.

I don't want to be a lazy person! I want to be diligent; I want to be wise and faithful with my time and the talents God has given me. I must push back daily on the Curse and choose to work. Work is good.

Today, I'm going to choose to be diligent. I'm going to choose to have authority over these lazy bones and accept the fact that life is hard and it wasn't meant to be easy. We live in a world wrapped in sin, and so we must fight; we must remain faithful. We press on, remembering the goal: *to live with eternity in mind.*

We work so there is order and so we can eat and live, but we also work so we can become like Jesus and love others well.

We choose to lift up our work to heaven. We choose to let the Holy Spirit have His way in us, making us humble and willing to *serve.* We choose to create beauty out of chaos in order to love those who need a soft place to land.

It really is all a choice—the choice to surrender to the One who will work through us.

I can relate to all of you out there who struggle with laziness and a lack of motivation to clean.

Like you, it's not that I don't like having a clean, peaceful home; it's that I find cleaning terribly boring. However, since cleaning is part of life, it must be done or life becomes chaotic and stressful (if not for us, for those around us). Here are some tips to help you get into perseverance mode (aka a cleaning groove):

- Read over your mission statement (you should probably do this every morning).
- "Put shoes on your feet," says the FlyLady.[1] I confirm that when I put on sneakers it actually helps—you feel like you should move when you have sneakers on.
- Do the hardest thing first. You know that chore that feels like a mountain? For me it's the kitchen . . . and laundry . . . and . . . Climb it before you do anything else. Once you "eat that frog" everything else will seem like a molehill.[2]
- Play music and dance while you clean.
- Get your kiddos involved and make it fun. Have a competition to see who can clean different rooms the fastest—and award some type of prize to the winner.
- Remind yourself how good it feels to be in a clean, inviting, peaceful environment.
- Consider the eternal value of your work.

Mary Challenge

 READ PROVERBS 6:10-11; 12:24; AND 13:4.

What are some blessings you can see in choosing to work rather than giving in to your lazy bones? List some on the lines provided.

Sarah Mae

MARTHA CHALLENGE

**TODAY YOU ARE TAKING CARE OF THE
SECOND BEDROOM'S CLOSET!**

 You can do it! Clear out that closet, give stuff away, PURGE, BABY, PURGE!

123

DAY 17

Finding Joy in the Self-Disciplined Life

Without discipline, there's no life at all.

KATHARINE HEPBURN

RISING SLOWLY INTO CONSCIOUSNESS, I hear a voice, a man's low voice. I don't know what he's saying. Wait . . . here they come, words and sentences. I turn my head toward my radio alarm clock: 6:00 a.m. My hand has a mind of its own, and before I can do anything about it, my fingers find the snooze button, press it down, and then quickly slide back under my pillow.

It's warm and I don't want to get up.

There's that voice again. Up, up, up . . . my eyelids open slowly: 6:09 a.m. "Okay, I'm up. I'm getting up."

I turn the sound of the radio alarm clock off and sit up. Time to get moving.

I've committed to getting up around 6 a.m. for the next few months as an experiment in getting my life in better order. It's been hard, but good. It helps that it's summer and the sun reaches in like a hand, taking mine and helping me up.

I have a routine: Make coffee, drink coffee, write in my journal, read my Bible, pour another cup of coffee.

I am finally awake.

It never feels worth it to get up when I'm lying in my cozy, warm bed, curled up in sleep, lost in a dream. But after the coffee and writing and reading, and time to get *sane* before the day really begins, I know it's worth it. The discipline of getting up early is changing my life because it changes my days. And of course, our days added up are our lives.

Choosing to get up early has been a discipline. It's not easy, and I don't always do it. In fact, in the winter, forget it. I'm sleeping in with my kiddos until 7:30 or 8:00 a.m. But I never regret when I do get up early; it's worth the struggle.

That's the thing with discipline—it's hard and often painful, but it's worth it. And in fact, we can find joy in it.

How do we live a joy-filled life of self-discipline?

On the following pages are some tips to help you on your journey toward a life of (imperfect) self-discipline.

Six Tips for Working toward a Self-Disciplined Life

1. *Make a commitment.* You have to be willing to commit to a lifestyle of submission to the Holy Spirit. Submission is not easy, and we will mess up, but we can hold on to our ideals of self-discipline while loosening our grip on the idea that we control our lives. God is molding us, and self-control, which goes hand in hand with self-discipline, is a fruit of the Spirit, so it will come in time as we bend our spirits to the One who does the changing.

2. *Set and complete goals.* This is important! Start small; don't say you're going to clean the whole house when you know you will get tired after forty-five minutes! My goal, for example, is to clean my kitchen every day by 9:00 a.m., and I intend to complete that one little goal. The reason I'm choosing that particular goal to work on is because I don't like cleaning my kitchen, so I want it out of the way before the day really begins. Don't get too wrapped up in the setting of goals unless you feel you can complete them—remember, one step at a time and a ton of grace!

3. *Do what you say you will do.* This has everything to do with integrity and trustworthiness. I want to be someone who follows through with what I say, but I've got to commit to doing it. Will you?

4. *Learn to say no.* If you can learn to say no, you will free up time and much unneeded stress. Seriously, this has helped me big time! If it's not a priority, or you're only doing it out of guilt, don't do it! Saying no is all part of time management, so say yes only if you know you can commit without your other priorities falling to the wayside.

5. *Practice.* Anyone who has learned a life of self-discipline will tell you it took time and practice. As we continue to work toward that goal, focusing on what lies ahead, we will naturally become more self-disciplined—but it takes hard work. Practice, practice, practice! Practice getting up early until it becomes a habit (or at least easier). Practice getting your kitchen cleaned before noon until it becomes second nature (okay, maybe that's a stretch). The point? Don't give up.

6. *Don't give up.* This says it all.

{ Mary Challenge }

READ GALATIANS 5:22-23

What will happen as we mature in the faith?

_____

_____

_____

_____

_____

_____

_____

_____

_____

_____

_____

_____

_____

_____

MARTHA CHALLENGE

TODAY MOVE TO THE THIRD BEDROOM! KEEP GOING!

You are *so* close to being done. And if you are done, happy dance! If you have much more to do, start planning a weekend to play catch-up. You will feel so good when the bedrooms are clean!

 ## *C'MON, WORK THAT MUSCLE*

Commit to doing one thing (only one) for one week. It can be as simple as "I will do ten jumping jacks every morning" or as challenging as "I will have no sugar for one week." Maybe you want to try getting up earlier in the morning or reading to your kids for forty-five minutes every day. I suggest something simple unless you are a real go-getter. The point is to build your self-discipline muscle!

DAY 18

Grace for Those Days

Only by trusting can we truly please God.

JOHN LYNCH, *THE CURE*

SO THERE IS DISCIPLINE, which is good and helpful and sturdy. It is tangible and measurable. And then there is this wild thing called *grace*.

Living a life of grace is when we hand all our good intentions to God and we say, "Please do something with these, Lord, because only You have the power to really change me."

Not too long ago I had a most profound revelation that changed my life. I had been striving to become a better cleaner, wife, mother, person, but it all came undone for me. I kept failing over and over again.

I thought, *Why bother? I'll just keep messing up anyway.*

This try-harder life wasn't working, and it was just making me feel lousy. I was watching myself get depressed, and eventually, I just gave up and stopped trying altogether.

And then, like a ray of light shining into the darkness of my failures, I remembered that I was just clay.

If I am clay, I will be nothing but a colorless lump unless I am picked up by God, the Potter. How silly of me to think I could mold myself. He is the One who does the molding, and I am the one who trusts His process and submits to it. How freeing that is!

There is no striving on my part to mold this lump any faster or better—or frankly, at all. No more striving or feeling guilty over my lack of change. He is taking care of me; He is kneading and forming and making something beautiful out of me.

I don't have to clean the kitchen every day to be good enough.

I don't have to have my bookshelves organized or my laundry put away to be good enough.

I am enough, already, in Christ.

And when I fail, which I will, my position in Christ, the love my Father has for me, and who I am do not change. My spirit is intertwined with His, and nothing can change that. When I fail or when I achieve, He loves me the same. He does the work.

Now when I clean and take care of my home, it is not because I have to in order to sidestep guilt or be a good homemaker. I do it because I have a place to care for and eternal souls to love. It is practical to clean, and it is necessary, but my identity has nothing to do with it.

My identity is not in being a wife, a mother, or a homemaker, or in any other calling or job. It is purely in Christ. He tells me who I am, and He loves me where I am.

This freedom of knowing that He is doing the work, and that the Holy Spirit is working even as I type, is almost too much to grasp—too grand, too beautiful. I am free because of His grace!

> *It was for freedom that Christ set us free; therefore keep standing firm and do not be subject again to a yoke of slavery.* GALATIANS 5:1
>
> *Without faith it is impossible to please God.*
> HEBREWS 11:6, NIV

We Need Him

Sometimes we miss spending time with God.

We are tired, life rushes us, we don't know where to start, we feel lost, we feel overwhelmed, and we don't have the time. A thousand reasons keep us from opening His Word. I know, I'm right there with you trying to figure out when I'm going to read and ingest His Word. I'm working on setting my alarm to get up early, but I am tempted to quit the moment the alarm goes off. I pound the snooze button as many times as I can, thinking, *Why do I want to get up early again? What's the benefit again?*

Once the day begins, I have to care for three little ones,

and we might read a Bible story together, but it isn't the true feasting that I desperately need. When there's a quiet moment in the day, I decide I'd rather get a certain job done or play around on social media. Evening comes and I'm tired, but maybe I'll write or just watch a movie with my husband. And then off to bed. Jesus is always with me, and I talk to Him throughout the day, but without His Word, I'm empty.

I need Him, my daily Bread, every day.

We all do—those of us who follow Him. I have a friend who tells me that when she can't seem to glean anything from the Word, especially in the early morning hours when she's tired and her brain is foggy, she chooses to offer the time to Jesus as worship. She'll read His Word as a gift to Him. I like that.

Even when we don't "feel" it, we can still let the Word in, and we can make it an offering to God.

Mary Challenge

READ PSALM 119:105 AND PROVERBS 6:23.

What happens when we read the Word?

_____

_____

_____

_____

_____

_____

_____

Read God's Word every day for five days straight—not because you have to, but because you can.

If you don't know where to start, try the book of Hebrews. Read one chapter of Hebrews every day for five days, and if you aren't gleaning anything, or you are still feeling spiritually dry, try telling yourself that this is your offering to God, your time in His Word whether you "feel" it or not.

MARTHA CHALLENGE

TODAY YOU HAVE ONE GOAL.

☐ *Wash all the bedding in the house that is being used.*

THAT'S IT. GO!

DAY 19

Fighting Fatigue

He tends his flock like a shepherd: He gathers the lambs in his arms and carries them close to his heart; he gently leads those that have young.

ISAIAH 40:11

SHE WAS FOUR MONTHS old when we lived with my in-laws.

Our little Ella, our firstborn, slept next to us in her Pack 'n Play, while we squeezed together in my in-laws' small bed. They gave us their room during the two months we were looking for a house.

Every few hours Ella would wake up, wanting to be fed. I would pull her into bed with us, holding her close so she wouldn't fall off the edge, and I would nurse her. She would get up at least two times a night. In the morning she woke up between 6:00 and 6:30, ready to eat again.

All I could think of was, *I am so tired.*

I just kept reminding myself that in two hours I could put her down for a nap and I could sleep too. It was that comforting thought that got me through the long, boring, tiring mornings. There isn't much you can do when you're not in your own home and watching over a baby.

Nap time came and was over too soon.

During this season of my life, beginning with Ella and continuing with two more children, I was almost always tired and brain depleted.

I'm telling you this because if you're a mom of small children, you may not be able to fight the fatigue. I'll offer you some suggestions, but know that it's okay to just be tired. There is no need to feel guilty for this, and there is grace for the season. Hang in there.

Even though the days of getting up to feed an infant in the middle of the night are behind me, that doesn't mean I jump out of bed at the crack of dawn. There are some mornings when I wake up feeling like a Mack truck hit me . . . then turned around and ran back over me. Ever had that feeling?

It doesn't matter how organized I am for the day, if I have my priorities staring me in the face, or if I have a routine to kick my behind in gear—when I'm tired, I'm useless.

Here are some energizing tips I've found that may help you push through your fatigue:

- *Move.* Apparently, inactivity makes you more tired. This means you need to do something such as walking, running, dancing with your kiddos, kickboxing, swimming, hiking, walking, or—(ta-da)—cleaning!

- *Only get the amount of sleep you need.* It turns out that I function much better on six to seven hours of sleep rather than eight. In fact, when I have more than eight hours of sleep, I'm like a sloth—I just want to sleep more! Figure out how much sleep you really need, and then get it. Try experimenting with your sleep patterns, keeping track of the times you lie down and wake up. Determine when you feel the most rested and try to stick with what works for you.

- *Increase your magnesium (this one's out of the blue!).* In a study in Grand Forks, North Dakota, the Human Nutrition Research Center of the Department of Agriculture found that women who had magnesium deficiencies had faster heart rates and needed more oxygen to do physical tasks than they did after their magnesium levels had been brought to recommended levels. The findings, says nutritionist Samantha Heller, show that lack of sufficient magnesium causes the body to work harder, and ultimately this can leave you feeling depleted.[1]

   "The recommended daily intake of magnesium is around 300 milligrams for women."[2] You can get magnesium from almonds, hazelnuts, or cashews as well as whole grains and fish.

- *Work on minimizing stress.* Remember how we talked about feeling overwhelmed? Well, work on the suggestions I gave you on Day 12 for overcoming feeling overwhelmed with what you have to do because evidently, stress makes you tired too.
- *Caffeine!* I am certainly not a nutritionist, but my number one suggestion if you're not prego or nursing is CAFFEINE! Allow yourself to indulge in some of it, preferably in coffee. Yum!

The Secret to Having Energy

With my hot cup of coffee next to me on the table while I'm sinking into my favorite chair, notebook on my lap and a pen in my hand, I can't write fast enough. Thoughts for the talk I'm preparing are pouring out over the page, one after another. I love when this happens.

When illumination and Scripture collide, a revelation is born. The sacred words breathe life, and their sharpness pierces the clouded places of my mind, giving me clear understanding. Of course, I want to share it! I want to speak this life into the women who will be gathering to hear it. I have the joy of speaking truth into the souls of women, and it makes me nearly burst with gratefulness and excitement.

Speaking gives me energy.

Aha! I have tapped into an energy-giving secret.

Are you ready for it? It's just so simple.

Allow yourself the freedom to do something you get jazzed about.

Seriously, that's it. And let me tell you, it works! Find something you thoroughly enjoy, something that makes you come alive, and then make time for it in your schedule. When I do this, I don't drag as much. In fact, I become a much more effective wife, mom, and homemaker.

So whatever it is that makes you come alive, carve out a couple of hours in your week and go for it!

Maybe you will even find yourself exploring how you can combine your jazzy activity with your main priorities. Wouldn't that be a lovely and energizing collision?

Mary Challenge

 READ ISAIAH 40:11 ·

According to this passage, what does God do for you? How
does knowing how the Lord treats those with young help
you give yourself more grace during times of fatigue?

_____

_____

_____

_____

_____

_____

_____

_____

_____

_____

_____

_____

_____

_____

What gets you jazzed? What makes you come alive? Write down some possibilities, whether they seem realistic or not, on the lines provided. Then begin to carve out some time to fill your soul in these creative ways.

 MARTHA CHALLENGE

TODAY WE ARE ON THE THIRD BEDROOM CLOSET!

 You've got this! And if you don't have a third bedroom, use this day
to catch up on another task.

DAY 20

Distractions

How soon "not now" becomes "never."

MARTIN LUTHER

I HAVE A PROBLEM.

I tend to get sucked into certain TV shows. On Netflix. Where you can watch them back-to-back. *Every night.*

First, it was *Felicity*, back when I was first married. A friend lent me her *Felicity* DVD set, and I watched almost all of it in a week.

Then there was the show *24*. My husband and I had only one little babe, and she went to bed at 6:30 every night. We had just moved into a new house and everything was in boxes. Instead of unpacking, we sat and watched all the episodes of *24* on DVD. We were seriously sleep deprived during this time, staying up each night until 2:00 a.m.

Fast-forward to this past fall when we got a streaming Netflix subscription. I found the show *Bones*, and proceeded to watch every episode within two months' time. As you can imagine, I didn't get much done during those months.

And you know what I've been doing the past two weeks? Watching *Felicity*. Again.

I know. It's sad, really. So sad, in fact, that I canceled my Netflix subscription because clearly my self-control levels are at an all-time low. With the canceled subscription and no access to any channels, I just lowered my distraction levels significantly. My husband is proud.[1]

There are a million and one things to distract us from being productive, and some are even good distractions (our children, our husbands). But we all know there are distractions that just kill our time and waste our lives. Yes, we all need to take a break sometimes to relax and let ourselves be distracted. But on the whole, distractions can really mess with us and keep us from living. Or just doing the things we need to do.

What is stealing the life from your productivity? What do you know you need to lay down the law about and get serious about walking away from? How are your time-redeeming skills?

Mary Challenge

READ PSALM 90:12

What does this verse say about our days and what we should do with them? Why does this matter?

_____

_____

_____

_____

_____

_____

_____

_____

_____

_____

_____

_____

_____

_____

_____

_____

MARTHA CHALLENGE

TODAY WE MOVE INTO THE DINING ROOM.

(If you don't have a dining room, you can take a day off or work on another cleaning project.) What needs to happen in your dining room to get it clean? Today we're doing that!

CLEAN ALL SURFACES

1. Clean off all surfaces; scrub them down or dust them.

2. Clean up clutter spots in the room and be *ruthless* when it comes to throwing out papers and things you don't need.

3. Once you've cleaned and organized, sweep and mop your floors or vacuum them.

   You are now ready for a lovely candlelit dinner with your family!

DAY 21

Limitations (Life Is Hard)

God is good, and life is worthwhile in spite of its pain. I
am regaining the joy of giving by accepting the pain and
struggle. I do all I can to alleviate my sufferings and those
of others. But even when pain and death do hold sway,
I am not utterly quenched or without hope. At the depths of
suffering, I keep finding Christ, who is there before me.

BARBARA MOUSER, *FIVE ASPECTS OF WOMAN*

BABIES, HOMESCHOOLING, SICK KIDDOS, depression, emergencies, exhaustion—all these things and more limit our ability to run our days according to our ideals.

For example, last night I set my alarm for 5:15 a.m. and went to bed with a smile on my face, fully planning to rise early and read my Bible. Guess what happened a little after 11:00 p.m.? My dear little boy got sick (the gross kind of sick). A bath, fresh blankets, and lots of love later . . . he did it again . . . *and again* (they never seem to hit the trash can!). Then my two-year-old woke up and would not go back to sleep. I finally faced reality and turned my alarm clock off. *Life happens.* We need to recognize our limitations and just accept them; the more we fight them, the more we bang our heads against a wall that isn't moving.

If you are struggling with pregnancy or depression, chasing after little ones, balancing job and home, etc., just do *something*. Make your bed, vacuum, put some flowers on your dining room table. Do one small thing to bring life to your home, even if you don't feel like you have much life in you at the moment.

I'm going to share with you something I wrote a while ago on one of my good days. It reminds me of what to look forward to—a future hope.

Some days when I wake up, I am so tired and I feel so gloomy . . . my spirit inside yearns for more, but my body halts me. Then there are days like today when I wake up and feel so fantastic physically and mentally! My giddiness totally pushes out the darkness of the day, and I hear the birds singing instead of the rain falling (although I do love the rain!). Why is this? Why can't I wake up ready to take on the day every day? Why is it that on days like today my coffee is only a supplement instead of a defibrillator, bringing me back to life? I want my life to be a light shining for my children . . . I want them to see a bouncy, jolly homemaker whizzing through her tasks with all the joy of the Lord! Boy, do I fall short! It's days like today that I glimpse what heaven will be like, when my body and its physical limitations and weariness will be but a shadow.

Just think, one day we will be free and unencumbered, and our joy will shine like the sun.

Mary Challenge

 READ 2 CORINTHIANS 12:9 ·

What happens to us when we are weak but rely on God?
What does He give us?

_____

_____

_____

_____

_____

Think of a limitation you have. It could be lack of sleep,
a disability, a circumstance—anything that makes you
feel limited in your ability to do all the things you'd like
to accomplish in a day. Now write it down on a piece of
paper, fold it up, offer it to God, and then throw it away.
No more guilt.

Let grace cover the areas you cannot change. Don't beat
yourself up or think you aren't doing enough. God knows
where you're at; His grace is sufficient.

 # MARTHA CHALLENGE

TODAY WE CLEAN THE KIDS' SCHOOL STUFF.

Let's clean and organize your homeschool space or the place where all of your children's school stuff is kept.

If you have a homeschool room, you will want to follow the steps for cleaning the living room (see Day 7). If you have a space such as a desk or a closet or a buffet cabinet or other area where you store your homeschool or school stuff, here is how we'll tackle that:

 ORGANIZE _____

1. Pull everything out.

2. Sort into piles: papers to keep, trash, items to organize, school books, school supplies, etc.

3. Clean the area—desk, closet, cabinet, or whatever you are using to store the school stuff.

4. Organize everything. If you need more bins or other types of containers, be sure to get them as soon as you can before things get jumbled again.

Ahhh . . . doesn't that feel better? Here's to learning!

DAY 22

Diligence
and Willing Hands

She seeks wool and flax, and works with willing hands.

PROVERBS 31:13, ESV

MY OLDEST HAD PASSED her swim test at the local pool with ease.

She's on the swim team, and on the first day of testing, she completed the requirements, gave me a high five, and then walked right over to the coveted deep end where those who passed were lining up for the diving board.

My youngest two looked at the diving board in awe, wishing so much they could use it. But both of them failed the test.

Over the next few days they tried again, but they just couldn't manage to swim the whole lap. It was discouraging for them and for me. Would they ever pass? Would they ever be able to reach their goal of jumping off the diving board?

Yes, they would, but it took hard work and determination to not give up.

My youngest passed the test before her brother. She practiced and practiced and listened as I showed her how to kick her legs and move her arms. She went over to the testing area, got the lifeguard, and began the test.

She didn't even make it halfway.

So she began to practice some more.

Before I could stop her, she was in the testing area again, but this time I could see that she was almost all the way across the pool! I went over and got to her just as she was getting out. "I did it, Mom! I did it!" She had swum all the way across! There was just one problem. She hadn't let the lifeguard know she was attempting it again, and he didn't see her. It didn't count. She would have to do it again.

She was exhausted, but instead of letting the news of her hard work not being seen or counted get her down, she rested. She got some pizza and enjoyed the sun. And about forty-five minutes later, she asked the lifeguard to watch and went for it again. And she passed—officially.

I was so proud of her.

As I high-fived her, I looked at my son and saw tears in his eyes.

I tried to encourage him and teach him, but he just kept saying, "It's too hard! I'll never do it!" There wasn't much I could do. I knew he needed inner resolve.

Well, he got that inner resolve once some teenagers took it upon themselves to take him under their wings and teach him. There were at least eight of them, mostly girls. They went to the testing area with him and worked with him and cheered him on and wouldn't let him give up. It was the coolest thing to see. After a long time of them helping him and telling him he could do it, he decided to take the test again.

He jumped in and started swimming, but about halfway through he started to go to the side. But wouldn't you know? Those teen coaches, all eight of them, wouldn't let him quit. They kept saying, "You can do it! You're halfway there! Keep going!"

He did as he was told. He kept swimming, and as he neared the end of the pool, the shouts got louder and louder; this accomplishment wasn't just his—it was theirs as well.

He got out of the pool with the biggest smile on his face. He did it. He passed.

When it comes to anything we want to accomplish, I have found that there are two things that are keys to our success:

1. Resolve and a willingness to work hard and be diligent
2. Not to go it alone

Even though it's hard to get motivated and be consistent when it comes to cleaning, do you have a willing heart to keep things clean? Do you have willing hands? Are you willing to give yourself to the work in order to build your vision?

If you're anything like me, you dream of the ideal that you will keep your home clean and organized every day. You'll get up early and do laundry, make breakfast, keep the kids in line with their chores. Oh, and you'll also be dressed, including a touch of lipstick for good measure.

But then your ideals fall flat. There have been many days when I've moaned, "I just can't keep it together!" The problem is not my inability to pursue my ideals; it's the fact that I stay stuck on the word *can't*.

I need to change my *can't* into *can*.

I *can* pursue my ideals, and I *can* do them (for the most part) consistently, with the Lord's help and grace. But first I need to have realistic ideals, goals that fit who I am. I will never be up early doing laundry with lipstick on. And that's okay! But I can work toward being consistent. I am healthy (praise God), I am able bodied, and I have the ability to practice self-discipline.

If I place value on the work, I am likely to do it. The point is, I *can* do the work; I just have to be realistic and kind to myself about how I will go about it.

I can follow through with my ideals. I can choose to let go of "perfect" and instead cling to "do something."

And when I feel like I can't, I can reach out for support or help. Just knowing we're not alone is a huge comfort, and having friends or a group of encouragers can give us the boost we need to keep on.

Are you with me?

Mary Challenge

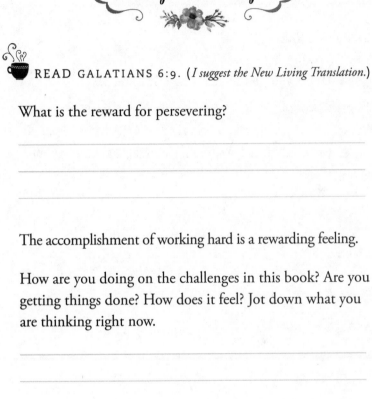

READ GALATIANS 6:9. (*I suggest the New Living Translation.*)

What is the reward for persevering?

_____

_____

_____

The accomplishment of working hard is a rewarding feeling.

How are you doing on the challenges in this book? Are you getting things done? How does it feel? Jot down what you are thinking right now.

_____

_____

_____

_____

Do you need to go slower or faster? Go at whatever pace you need to. The point is not to compete, but to complete.

 MARTHA CHALLENGE

SORTING DAY!

SETTLE IN AND SORT

Remember how you stuffed all those papers and miscellaneous items from your kitchen counters and drawers into a bag or bin? Well, friend, today is the day you are going to sort through all of that stuff. Yep. So settle in with some good tunes and get to it!

DAY 23

Time

The bad news is time flies. The good news is you're the pilot.

MICHAEL ALTSHULER

"SOMETIMES WHEN I'M AROUND people, I still feel lonely."

My oldest curls up on the couch as she says those words. I leave my comfy chair, go over to her, kneel down, and begin to rub her back. "Want to tell me about it?"

I listen as she moves and sits up and a light shines in her eyes. "I just want to go on a date with you. When can we go on a date?" Oh yes, the date I promised her we'd go on, the date I forgot about, the date I needed to mark down so it's set. Her love language is quality time, and when I'm not

giving that time to her, she feels lonely and lost and sad. I
tell her I will talk to Daddy about a good night to go out.
She smiles.

I've got to make time for that date.

But there's the cleaning and the cooking and the writing,
and school lessons, and commitments, and . . .

This is not life. Life is full when children are taken on
dates, families spend Saturdays together, books are read
slowly, food is shared with the hurting, adventures are
embarked upon, and laundry is folded with little hands who
need to learn. I choose this.

Time is mine for the molding. *I choose . . .*

> whether or not to sit with my children during breakfast
> and talk with them.
> whether or not to wrap my children in blankets with me
> and read.
> whether or not to turn off the TV.
> whether or not to play cards with my son, or draw
> with my daughter, or read book after book with
> my littlest one.
> whether or not to go to bed early with my husband.
> whether or not to use my time wisely when it comes
> to writing and planning and traveling.

I choose. *The time is mine to use.*

Sometimes choosing to go out on a date with your child
is the best choice.

Sometimes washing the dishes with your child, gently teaching him or her, is the best choice.

Sometimes letting the house stay messy for a time so you can go to the park with your kids is the best choice.

There is only so much time, so we need to choose what we do wisely.

Doing the Math

Have you ever felt like you have a billion things to do but not enough time to do them? (Just for fun, let's put a billion in perspective: One billion seconds ago it was 1983. One billion minutes ago—are you ready for this one?—the apostle John, the last of the original twelve, died!)

I always catch myself saying, "If only I had more time!" There are so many things in life I want to do and be, but I feel stifled by the restraints of time. But you know what? I don't use my time wisely. I am a slave to time, and I have allowed it to be stolen from me more times than not. What a waste!

> *Teach us to number our days,*
> *that we may gain a heart of wisdom.*
> PSALM 90:12, NIV

I decided to number my days, and I discovered that if I live until I'm seventy-seven (a nice biblical number), I have forty-two years left on this earth (or 504 months; 2,190 weeks; 15,330 days—I have already been alive for 12,775 days). How am I going to use what I have left?

How are you going to use what you have left?

We are never going to find more time, which is why the apostle Paul encourages us to be vigilant.

I like what Chuck Swindoll says: "God has given you . . . sufficient time in each day for you to fulfill His perfect plan—including the interruptions!"[1]

I never looked at it that way! Here I am complaining that there is not enough time in each day (i.e., life), when what I'm really doing is saying, "God, You didn't know what You were doing when You created time on this earth." The truth is that He knows exactly what He's doing, and He knows exactly how much time we need to accomplish His purposes. Talk about a renewed perspective!

Mary Challenge

 READ EPHESIANS 5:15-16 ·······················

There are two options for who we choose to live like.
What are they? What does God tell us to do through this
Scripture?

_____

_____

_____

_____

_____

_____

_____

_____

_____

_____

_____

George MacDonald is credited as saying, "Like a budget for money, you need a budget for time." How are you budgeting yours? Take an honest appraisal of your time.

_____

_____

_____

_____

_____

Figure out how much time you have left on this earth if you live until you are seventy-seven. I suggest calculating it in the number of days. Write that number down.

_____

Now, the critical question: What are you going to do with your remaining days? Jot down some thoughts.

_____

_____

_____

_____

_____

MARTHA CHALLENGE

CLOSETS!

 *Today we are taking on the remaining closets in our homes, such as a coat closet.*

Get rid of things you do not need. Keep only what you actually use. Less stuff = less stress.

DAY 24

Help! To Hire or Not to Hire

*She rises while it is yet night and gets [spiritual] food for
her household and assigns her maids their tasks.*

PROVERBS 31:15, AMPC

SHE CAME, SHE SCRUBBED, she vacuumed, she washed
. . . *she was my hero.*

Missy came every week to bless me with her cleaning
skills. She saw the worst of my cleaning ability and lack
thereof. She was a gift to our family for the time we had her.
And I didn't feel guilty one bit.

But there was a time I did.

There was a time I thought having help meant I wasn't a
good enough homemaker.

Let me tell you something: That's just plain silly.

There is nothing wrong with hiring some help if you are able to do so.

Seriously, where did all the guilt and shame come from when it comes to wanting (needing?) a little help around the house? Granted, if you can't afford it, that's life—and God will give you the grace you need to get through. But if you can afford it (and your husband is cool with it), then I say go for it. If I could, I would have someone come once a week to help out!

Here's a perspective from organizer Blair Massey that I find incredibly helpful whenever I feel sorry for myself:

I remember when it hit me that the Proverbs 31 woman had maids working for her. I thought, "How unfair it is that she had maids and I have to do all this work on my own (pout, pout)."

Then the Lord opened my eyes. He helped me realize how many maids I actually had! There was the washing machine and dryer, the vacuum cleaner, the dishwasher, the microwave, the slow cooker, the oven, the toaster, the coffee pot, and my favorite— the bread machine. When I stopped to think about it, all my appliances were performing services just like the maids of the Proverbs 31 woman. How convicting. No more pouting for me![1]

Mary Challenge

 READ 2 PETER 1:3

What do we have to help us in this life? Spend some time in prayer, thanking God for all the "help" you do have. Jot down a list on the lines provided.

For the areas in your life in which you feel you're drowning, ask Him to show you where you can find some help.

MARTHA CHALLENGE

TODAY WE WILL BE CLEANING THE FAMILY ROOM,
or whatever extra room you have in your home that needs some cleaning!
If you don't finish this room today, no worries. You can complete it on
a Saturday or the catch-up project day on Day 30.

FAMILY ROOM CLEANING

Don't forget to fill those Goodwill boxes!

DAY 25

The Thing We All Have in Common

When you aim for perfection, you discover it's a moving target.

GEORGE FISHER

I DID IT AGAIN.

I compared myself to her. I kept thinking, *She is smarter, prettier, and funnier, and her house is always clean and orga- nized and decorated just so. I wish I was like her. I wish my house looked like hers.*

I wish I could just get it together. Will I ever?

Here's the deal: No one has it all together, not even my superorganized cleaning friend I've been wishing I was.

She is not perfect, I am not perfect, and neither are you. And that's okay.

Deep sigh of relief.

So, what's all the fuss over getting it all together? Life is just one big faith step we take one day at a time. We are all just walking it out, doing our best as we fight a sin-saturated world that pushes hard against us. Give yourself a break, friend. You're not alone in your struggles or your feelings of failure. And you don't have to be good enough. Your worth does not lie in your ability to clean well; your worth and value lie in Christ alone.

I agree with author Harriet Braiker's observation: "Striving for excellence motivates you; striving for perfection is demoralizing."[1] Let's be motivated.

Mary Challenge

 READ HEBREWS 10:14. (*If you have an ESV Bible, read it there.*)

The word *perfect* means "complete." How does knowing what this Scripture teaches encourage you as you live out this life?

_____

_____

_____

_____

_____

_____

_____

_____

_____

_____

_____

_____

_____

_____

_____

_____

Think about some areas in your life where you have been striving to be perfect. Perhaps you are comparing yourself to another mom, or putting unnecessary burdens on yourself because of what someone has said. Write down your thoughts on the lines provided.

Now take these thoughts in prayer to God and ask Him to replace any lies you believe with the truth.

 MARTHA CHALLENGE

TODAY WE ARE CLEANING THE ENTRYWAY IN OUR HOMES.

🌱 ENTRYWAY CLEANING _____

1. Get all the shoes, trash, junk, and whatever else you have scattered in your entryway, and put/throw it away. Set aside one pair of shoes per person to put back after you've cleaned.

2. Now sweep up the area and wash or vacuum it. Neatly line up the shoes.

3. If you have a coatrack, tidy that up as well, keeping only what you need.

4. Mail and keys area? Yep, take care of that, too!

The High-Low Cycle

We can rejoice, too, when we run into problems and trials, for we know that they help us develop endurance. And endurance develops strength of character, and character strengthens our confident hope of salvation. And this hope will not lead to disappointment. For we know how dearly God loves us, because he has given us the Holy Spirit to fill our hearts with his love.

ROMANS 5:3-5, NLT

RAISE YOUR HAND IF you've cleaned for a week or two straight, keeping everything in order and your kitchen clean, then *bam*—you're back to your messy ways.

Me too.

I call this the high-low cycle. You get on a high and manage to maintain your home for a little while, and then before you know it, your old ways creep back in and you are back at square one. How demoralizing is this cycle?! Here's the truth of the matter: You will most likely deal with this cycle the rest of your life.

You were hoping I'd have a quick fix for you, weren't you? Sorry, no can do. (Or if there is, I haven't found it yet. Have any of you?)

Here is what I do know: We are called to persevere . . . and to hope.

Hope keeps me going, the hope of something better one day. Everything we are doing to care for our families by way of our homes, we are doing for an eternal purpose! It all matters! God is maturing us with every spill lovingly cleaned up, every mouth wiped and diaper changed and kiss given and every other thing we do.

It matters and it is not insignificant. Your work in the mundane is refining you. Keep on, sister! At the end of it all, you're going to shine like gold.

Mary Challenge

☕ READ HEBREWS 6:10 ·······················

Think about this: Who sees the work you do day in and day out in your home?

_____

_____

_____

_____

_____

_____

_____

_____

Pay attention to the times of the month when you have more energy and are motivated to clean. For three months, write down how you feel each day on a calendar; after that time, see if you notice a pattern. Perhaps you can better prepare for your days if you know what's coming.

MARTHA CHALLENGE

CLEAN THE OFFICE.

Today we are cleaning out either a home office or the place where you keep all your paperwork.

FIRST, SORT PAPERS

Get all the papers out of your desk and begin to sort! Throw things away and make piles for what needs to go where. This is a good time to reevaluate your paperwork organization system. Do you need bins or folders or other kinds of storage?

If you find you have drawings and notes from your kids or friends and family, consider using a plastic bin with a lid or a separate folder in your filing cabinet to keep those special memories safe.

DAY 27

Laundry Blues

A load a day keeps chaos away.

FLYLADY

IT WAS SO BAD I decided it would be easier to burn than clean.

I was looking at the laundry.

Clothes everywhere. Piles and piles. Standing in the middle of the mounds, I thought, *Maybe that's why Steve Jobs wore the same black turtleneck and jeans every day. He could go for days if he needed to, and no one would notice if they were clean or not.*

Wouldn't it be so much easier to just go through, say, five outfits a week? Seems like a good idea to me! Burning everything? Too dangerous with children around. But seriously, all those clothes? It was not going to work for me anymore. It was time for a change.

With garbage bags in hand, I took care of business in that laundry room, and when I was done, I had *five* bags full of clothes to get rid of (some to Goodwill, washed first; some to the trash, not washed). While I'm not actually doing the five outfit thing, I have significantly reduced our clothing load, and it is glorious.

Are your clothes wrinkled from sitting in the basket after coming out of the dryer?

Do you have a hard time getting your clothes from the basket to the closet and dresser drawers?

Has your laundry basket become the go-to place for clean clothes?

If so, my friend, you may be suffering from what I call LBS—Laundry Basket Syndrome.

And girl, you've got to get ahold of this problem and nip it in the bud!

I know, because this is what I do. I put the laundry in the washer, then the dryer, and finally into the laundry basket assuring myself, "I'll get to that later." But I never do. A few days go by, and we're living out of the laundry basket, but the shirt I want to wear is wrinkled. Since I don't like to iron, I just find something else—and the cycle continues. I usually just end up washing all the clothes again because they get dumped out and I don't know what's clean or dirty anymore.

I know it's my fault, but I still feel like the laundry mocks me. "It will never end . . . *muhahahaha.*"

It's true, laundry will never come to an end, so I had better find myself a new perspective on my so-called nemesis. In fact, I think I will stop using the word *nemesis* in the same sentence as *laundry*. It's time for a perspective check.

"Thank You, Jesus, that my family has clothes to wear."

We have a lot of clothes. You know how it is—clothes, like bunnies, just multiply. I am sure if I were to just quit with the "Oh, but that is just too cute, I can't get rid of it" mentality, I would have much less laundry on my hands and all over my floor.

Here's the deal: I believe thankfulness goes a long way and we need to have grateful hearts when it comes to our things, but I also think there is a reality at play that just makes taking care of our things very difficult. What's a gal to do when it comes to taming the laundry beast? The number one answer seems to be "Do one load a day." You already knew that though, didn't you? Now you just have to do it.

And for good measure, try on some of these fabulous tips from fellow everyday mamas:

 READER'S TIPS⎯⎯⎯⎯⎯⎯⎯⎯⎯⎯⎯⎯

Get socks that are all one color. The girls have white socks and the boys have black ones. This makes sorting much easier.

Have a family closet. All the clothes are in one.

Have only a few outfits each. This has been the biggest help with laundry.[1]

–Renee Stam

When all the children were still at home, they each had a day for their laundry. If it wasn't brought up to the laundry room by 10:00 a.m., I no longer did it and they had to.[2]

—Kari Andres Kentner

Delegate, delegate, delegate! If the children are old enough to be able to unscrew the detergent cap and retain the knowledge of how to run the machines in my house, they're old enough to do their own laundry . . . even the short one![3]

—Liz Miller

For me, getting laundry washed isn't the problem, it's folding it all and putting it away (plus I would have to redo the folding often because the kids would dig through their drawers to find what they wanted). Now, each child has his or her own clean basket. When clothes come out of the dryer I sort them into each child's basket (I match the socks because they are too hard to find). I do not fold them or put them away. When the kids are instructed to go get dressed (or put on pajamas) they go to their baskets and pick out what they need. The exceptions are my clothes, my husband's, and dresses/dress shirts. Those get hung or folded.[4]

—Angela McKenzie

I used to get overwhelmed by laundry, then I traveled to Ethiopia in January of 2011. My perspective changed drastically! We visited a school located in a tiny village in the southern part of the country. The clothing we saw was extremely worn and dirty (there are no natural water sources and limited wells so clothing doesn't get washed). We were told that the clothing people wore was most likely the only clothing they owned. We were at the school for five days and the morning of day three I realized that the staff had been wearing the same clothing all three days. I wondered if it was all they owned. Yep, on days four and five they showed up wearing the same

shirts. It humbled me and laundry. . . . God showed me how MUCH I have
and the ugly sin of discontentment that was in my life.[5]

–Ingrid

I do one load at a time and don't start another until the first load is dried
and folded. That way, I don't get too overwhelmed by the mountains.[6]

–Keri Howell

I have four kids, ages nine to thirteen. Each kid has a laundry day during
the week. If they bring me all of their laundry (including their sheets and
towels) that morning before school, I wash and dry it. They have to fold it
and put it away after school. If they fail to bring it to me in the morning,
they have to do their own laundry another time during the week when they
could be doing something fun. This idea may not have worked with my kids
when they were younger, but it sure makes my life easier now![7]

–Jay Bee

I love using the delayed start on my washing machine. I put the clothes in at
night and delay the wash until the early morning, which means by the time I
wake up a load is done![8]

–Rachel Fry Ronning

At our house, we do "laundry stew." I dump a pile of clean clothes on the
family room floor and give each child a laundry basket. They sort and fold
their clothes while watching a movie or episode of *Little House on
the Prairie*. After they sort and fold, they put their laundry away. My
kids are four, eight, and eleven. They love it because it's a game to them,
and they get to watch a special show. They've been doing this since around
the age of three. It's easy, fun, and efficient![9]

–Mary Davies VonRosenburg

Mary Challenge

READ PSALM 51:7 ·

Is there anything you need to ask God to clean up in your heart right now? Add it to the lines provided.

_____

_____

_____

_____

_____

_____

_____

_____

Are you guilty of LBS? Find a laundry routine that works for you and your family. Perhaps you will implement one of the tips listed in this chapter or come up with your own.

MARTHA CHALLENGE

TODAY IS LAUNDRY ROOM DAY!

We are going to clean our laundry rooms and get some of those piles of clothes that are on the floor washed and put away!

LET THE FUN BEGIN

1. Sort the laundry and begin washing a load.

2. Clean off and wash the surfaces of the washer and dryer.

3. Take out any trash.

4. Vacuum or sweep the laundry room.

5. Tidy up any other areas necessary to make the room clean.

6. Go nuts! Sort, wash, and most important, *put it all away*!

DAY 28

Who Are You Trying to Please?

FROM SALLY CLARKSON'S
SEASONS OF A MOTHER'S HEART

I LOVE ENTERTAINING, SO I was really pleased with how everything looked on the day of the open house. The living areas were decorated with bright greens and reds of Christmas, a table full of lovingly prepared Christmas delicacies greeted our guests, the lighted candles and the fire in the fireplace added a warmth to the room, and the melodies of familiar Christmas music filled the room. It was such a lovely festive atmosphere that it made me forget all about our bedroom in the back stacked floor-to-ceiling with all the leftover stuff that had cluttered the house.

All went well with the open house until a small group of

friends reminded me of the one room that wasn't quite yet done. They asked, "Can we sneak back to see the rest of the house?" What could I say but, "Sure, as long as you promise to overlook the piles that we haven't gotten to yet!" I gave them a guided tour down the hallway. They were admiring the sweet home the Lord had provided for our family when we finally reached my overloaded bedroom. Someone commented how nice and large our bedroom was, and then it happened. The unraveling began.

One of my friends casually commented that when she had moved into her house an older woman had given her some advice. This woman said that if you really love your husband, and want to show him that he has first priority in your life, then you will make your bedroom the first place you organize and decorate. Ouch! That one simple comment cut straight to my heart and pierced it. She was right! It was obvious I had not paid any attention to our bedroom. I hadn't been thinking of Clay at all, only myself and getting my home in order.

I felt a deep stab of guilt as I realized how I surely must have disappointed my dear husband over the past two months. I had labored so hard to make my house nice, yet I had neglected his needs. What must he think of me? Why hadn't I seen what I was doing? I felt like the wind had been knocked out of me. Whatever good feelings I had about my new home started to unravel within me. After several days of feeling heavy-hearted and discouraged, I decided to tell Clay how sorry I was that I had not been a better wife.

I brewed him a cup of his favorite tea and sat down with

him on the couch. I reviewed the past two months, then explained what my friend had said and how it had cut me to the heart. I apologized to him for not being more sensitive to him, and for neglecting our bedroom for so long. I promised I would give it my highest priority immediately. I waited for a reply that would confirm my concerns.

Clay looked at me with a puzzled expression and said, "What in the world are you talking about?" I thought maybe he didn't understand how I had offended him so I explained it all again. He touched my shoulder and very matter-of-factly said, "Honey, it doesn't bother me at all that our bedroom is a mess. What's important to me is to have the main areas of the house neat and orderly. When they feel settled and homey, then I feel good about life. I really appreciate everything you've done to turn this house into our home. I know we'll get to the bedroom eventually. You've done a great job!"

I felt an immediate sense of relief from the guilt I had been feeling. But that was followed by an equal measure of indignation as I realized what had happened to me. Without even knowing it, I had judged myself guilty by someone else's standard. I had condemned myself by that standard and was left feeling like a complete failure. To my family and loved ones I was doing just fine, yet I was blinded to that fact by my own self-induced guilt.

Mary Challenge

 READ ROMANS 8:1 ···

What does this Scripture say about those who are
in Christ Jesus?

_____

_____

_____

_____

_____

_____

Are there areas in your life where you are experiencing
a burden of unnecessary guilt? Write some of those areas
on the lines provided.

_____

_____

_____

_____

Now ask your husband or someone else you trust and who knows you well to look at what you've jotted down and give you his or her perspective on what you've said. It could be an eye-opening exercise for you.

 MARTHA CHALLENGE

TODAY WE ORGANIZE THE KITCHEN!

Do you have a junk drawer in your kitchen? Okay, maybe you give it a fancier name such as the drawer of miscellanies or the mystery drawer. Maybe you have more than one. That catchall drawer is what we're cleaning today.

 HERE'S THE PLAN _____

1. Pull everything out of the drawer(s) you want to clean and organize. Go crazy!

2. If you find Christmas cards, throw them away—unless they really mean something to you and you must keep them. If you keep them, put them in a box labeled "Christmas cards."

3. As you're cleaning, be sure to have a bag or a bin for all the paperwork you're not sure what to do with yet (like the stack you took off the counter earlier and threw in a drawer). You can go through that later. For now, the goal is to clean and organize what you do want and need in the kitchen.

What I Would Say to My Younger Self about Cleaning

I'm not messy. I'm organizationally challenged!

GARFIELD

I USED TO REALLY beat myself up over the way my home looked, and I believed some lies that caused havoc in my heart. Lies that sounded like this:

"I will never change."
"My husband would be happier with a woman who cleaned all the time."
"I hate cleaning, and I hate that I'm not the cleaning type."

I put a lot of stock into how well and how often I cleaned (which wasn't well or often), and I constantly felt like a failure. I wanted to be a good homemaker; I wanted to make my husband proud.

It's been twelve years since I got married and started keeping a home, and while I've grown into my own as a homemaker, I still have to work at it. But I have learned a few things, and I'd like to share them with my younger self . . . and all the noncleaners of the world who struggle with feelings of failure.

Dear Younger Self,

Your identity is not defined by how well or how often you clean.

The sum of who you are is not in your ability to keep the dishes off the counter and the laundry put away. You are no less or no better in God's eyes. You are His, which means that you are beautiful and perfect because of Jesus, right now, right where you are. As you continue to submit to the Holy Spirit, He molds and changes you to be more like Jesus, and we are His. From an eternal perspective, we are already complete.

My friend, your identity is not in what your husband or anyone else thinks of you.

I used to believe the lie that my husband would be better off with someone who was a good cleaner. I was in so much bondage due to this lie; I felt worthless. The truth is, my husband would love it if I cleaned more and better, but he loves me and is committed to me for life. He accepts my purple boots, my sparkly nail polish (Can a grown woman wear sparkly nail polish? Yes!), my driven personality, and my complete lack of Martha Stewart DNA. I care what he thinks because I love him and respect him, but we also respect each other as we grow. The thing is, even if my husband thought I was worthless or stupid or whatever because I didn't clean up to a particular standard, it wouldn't really matter because he doesn't have the authority to tell me who I am. That authority is reserved for the throne of grace alone.

Only Jesus has the authority to tell me who I am.

You are not a slave to your personality.

I've got news for you, love— "This is just who I am, accept it" is a selfish excuse and not fit for a woman who longs to be like Jesus. When I claim, "This is me, deal with it!" I am not claiming the humility or servanthood of the One who died for all my ugly. No, that's not the way of the Cross. The way of the Cross is to submit your personality and your bent and all of the things that make you who you are to Jesus. All of who you are is for His glory.

It's okay to know you will never have the Martha Stewart way about you. God doesn't love you any more or any less because of your bents. However, He does ask you to obey, to be diligent, and to be like Jesus. And so I counsel you to practice laying yourself low and to follow the Way.

You can choose to love well through keeping your home.

I know you don't like to clean—you find it boring, and you'd rather do almost anything else. But listen, you can love others well by creating a place of peace and beauty for those around you. You can love yourself well by taking care of your home and giving life to it. You can create beauty out of ashes, peace out of chaos. It is Kingdom work, eternal work, because love is eternal. Look at cleaning as an act of love toward yourself and those around you. Look at it as an act of worship to your God, an ebb and flow of life that you will settle into.

I think the best part of being married, having children, and keeping my home is that I now understand more of who I am and that life undulates as I swim through it. I know the ups and downs, and I know there are times of great consistency, great upheaval, and great peace. I have learned to be content with the ebb and flow of life. I know I'll never be the go-go-go type of cleaner, but I also know I will care for my home and the people in it. I will choose to maintain my home, push back on the Genesis Curse, and persevere in order to love well.

It's a good place to be when you find peace, when you accept who you are, when you quit striving, and when you give yourself to the Potter. It's the sweet spot.

With love, Your Future Self

Mary Challenge

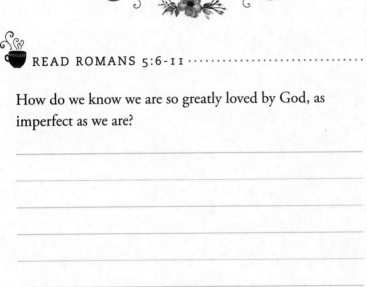

READ ROMANS 5:6-11

How do we know we are so greatly loved by God, as imperfect as we are?

_____

_____

_____

_____

_____

_____

_____

_____

_____

_____

Consider writing a letter to your younger self on what you've learned as a homemaker and what advice you'd give yourself to be free and loved and accepted for who you are. On the lines provided, jot down some of the ideas that you want to include. Then write your letter on a separate piece of paper.

_____

_____

_____

_____

_____

_____

_____

_____

_____

_____

_____

_____

_____

_____

_____

_____

Meditate on Hebrews 10:14. Ask God to show you what it means for you to be complete/perfect in Christ.

MARTHA CHALLENGE

TODAY WE ARE CLEANING OUT THE CABINETS AND THE TOP OF THE FRIDGE!

Don't fret—you are not pulling out all the dishes and dusting the cabinets. This only pertains to the cabinets that you know need to be organized. You know, the cabinet that has all the random stuff in it? Clean that one.

Make sure to also clean the top of your fridge.

Contentment in Your Season of Life

Since, then, you have been raised with Christ, set your hearts on
things above, where Christ is, seated at the right hand of God.
Set your minds on things above, not on earthly things.

COLOSSIANS 3:1-2, NIV

IT IS SO EASY to compare ourselves with others, isn't it?

Just last week I felt the monster of envy when I saw pictures of a friend's house and how she had decorated it so beautifully. And not only was it clean—it was spotless. I felt sad.

I shared my feelings of discontent with my mother-in-law, who graciously reminded me that my friend didn't have children. She also encouraged me to remember my season of life, to keep my mind on heavenly things, and to thank God for all the blessings He has given me.

Her counsel is wise and kind. We are all in different seasons of life, and for some of us that means not having the things we'd like or being able to order our homes exactly the way we would like.

If you find yourself depressed or angry about not being able to have the home you so desire, might I suggest that perhaps you are trying to find life in something other than the Life-Giver? He is the only One who can give us life; our worth and value come from Him alone.

Enjoy the seasons God allows you to move through and pray for a contented spirit.

Join me in embracing another wise counselor's words at the end of Proverbs, a book whose message is that real wisdom is based on a relationship with God.

Mary Challenge

☕ **READ PROVERBS 30:8-9**

Would you be willing to pray this prayer? Why or why not?

_____

_____

_____

_____

Write down ten things you are thankful for today.

_____

_____

_____

_____

_____

_____

_____

_____

_____

MARTHA CHALLENGE

PROJECT DAY!

What didn't you finish? What project have you been wanting to take on? Today, get to it!

DAY 31

Balancing It All

Love never fails.

I CORINTHIANS 13:8

BEING A LOVING WIFE, being an intentional parent, caring for our homes, and taking care of all the other commitments we hold close can seem impossible to balance.

I have a tendency to put each commitment in a figurative box and focus solely on that particular commitment. When I work only on that single box, I neglect everything else. But if I see life as a whole, I can see the puzzle pieces of life emerge into a picture of meaningful connectedness.

Life becomes a routine made up of the little intentional

things I choose to do throughout the day. I focus on one day at a time, leaning into faith and keeping my mind on the hope that is at the end of my journey. I choose to forgo perfection.

What keeps a household running well and in balance? *Love.*

Instead of striving to be a perfect wife, I will choose to kiss my husband before he leaves for work.

Instead of striving to be a perfect mother, I will choose to giggle with my kiddos throughout the day.

Instead of striving to accomplish my ideals, I will choose instead to let them gently guide me.

Instead of striving to change myself, I will choose to let the living Word of God change me from the inside out according to His timing and plan. I'll just keep my eyes on Him.

Mary Challenge

 READ PSALM 16:8

What happens when we keep our focus on God?

_____

_____

_____

_____

_____

_____

Kiss your husband, giggle with your kiddos, and do
a happy dance!

MARTHA CHALLENGE

REST. YOU'VE DONE A GREAT JOB!

And then after you rest, begin again.
Here's to (mostly) clean homes that are filled with love!

Is Messiness
a Morality Issue?

NO, I DON'T THINK it is.

But it could be.

Could there be a sin of laziness stemming from selfishness? Could there be a wall in your heart against cleaning because you feel you're being taken advantage of by those around you? Do you perhaps envy those who have a cleaning service, and therefore resent that you have to clean? All these issues are rooted in sin.

I think we should pull back the curtains of our hearts and find out what is there. Are we lazy or just tired? Being tired is not a sin! We need to be willing to be vulnerable and understand our strengths and our limitations, our sin issues and our bents. Whether you like to clean or don't, whether you are good at it or not doesn't really matter. What matters is what is in your heart.

Do you have a sin issue or a core lie you need to ask God to help you to deal with when it comes to your attitude toward taking care of your domain? If so, then perhaps messiness *is* a moral issue for you.

For many of us, I think we just get wrapped up in the "you should do" and the "you shouldn't do" and we forget to ask God, "Lord, who do You say I am? What do You say when it comes to caring for my home?" We need to approach the throne of grace if we are going to walk in grace and be instruments of grace; we need to be open to being healed or corrected.

You may be a messy person, and that may or may not be a moral issue for you. I'm asking you to ask God today if there is an issue you need to confront, or if you are just messy and need to persevere while not beating yourself up for who you are.

Cleaning is just a detail. I don't care if you are Miss Super Cleaner Lady or Miss Messy Pants, your cleaning personality has nothing to do with the identity of your soul. So whoever you are, wherever you are, let the details lead you to the state of your heart. I'm saying let the care of your domain come from a heart that overflows with love. Clean and maintain your home in order to push back the chaos and offer a place of rest and peace. Let it all be from the heart.

And from the heart—a redeemed heart—we can really love well.

A Word about Guilt

GUILT.

It flattens a spirit like a bag of bricks thrown on your back. Guilt slows you down, sometimes paralyzing you, wrecking your life. I'm talking about the guilt that taunts, "You are a failure; you will never get it together."

So we move slowly, aching all the way, heaped up in our failure for not doing all that we should be doing. We squirm in our skin because we want to please God, but why bother? We'll just keep messing up. "I want to keep trying, but there's no point. I'm just a mess."

Gobs of fleshy, glorious, God-image messes, that's what we are.

Guilt says, "Keep trying to get out of that mess (snicker); you never will. Try harder anyway. Oh, and you are disappointing God."

Quiet that slithering voice of guilt for a minute and hear this truth: You, with unveiled face (He sees you, He knows you!), are being transformed into His image by His Spirit.

We all, who with unveiled faces contemplate the Lord's glory, are being transformed into his image with ever-increasing glory, which comes from the Lord, who is the Spirit.   2 CORINTHIANS 3:18, NIV

Your soul stands naked before Him, and there is no shame if you are in Christ Jesus. He sees you and He sees Jesus because your spirits are welded together. And He loves you. We are all a mess. We will all fail.

Stand up straight.

Let the bricks fall off your back.

Put one foot in front of the other and walk. You have the strength and the power of the Universe Painter inside you. He will, by His spirit, change you and mold you, in time, for His glory. You just walk it out in freedom.

You can't lose His love.

So keep walking and give your spirit permission to breathe. *You are free.*

Ten Quick Tips for the Decorating Challenged

by Logan Wolfram

1. Paint Color Matters

When in doubt, put a neutral color on the walls and use color in the accessories. My personal favorites from the past few years (spanning 2012–2015) are Benjamin Moore Revere Pewter, Bleeker Beige, and Edgecomb Gray. When in doubt, those choices are a great place to start if they are still available.

The thing is, if you buy cheaper accessories (throw pillows, decorative boxes, baskets, etc.) you won't feel bad about changing them when you get tired of them in a few years. Plus, it's easier to switch them around periodically (although paint color is the easiest way to refresh a room!).

2. Rob Peter to Pay Paul

My mom always said it that way, but what it really means is go through your own house and shop it. Walk around and look for different things that you like in your own house. Go into a bunch of rooms and look for interesting things like boxes, accessories, jars, plants, vintage-looking toys, containers . . . anything. Put everything on a table and spread it out—this will help you see your things with new eyes. Regroup things. Take things that weren't together and make new vignettes. You're on your way to creating your own Anthropologie-looking display—trust me on this one!

3. Decorate with Books

Find some hardback books and remove the dust jackets so you can see the actual book, which sometimes is very pretty. You can turn books sideways and stack things on top of them, like a candle or a jar, for height. If you turn the book vertically it can become a frame for other things. My most favorite books that have gorgeous covers and are typically pretty cheap are *Reader's Digest* anthologies from the 1940s to 1980s. *So* pretty and easy to snag at thrift stores and on eBay!

4. Group Things in Odd Numbers

This is just a simple rule of thumb that makes your décor more appealing. Put things in groups of one, three, five, etc.

5. Buy What You Like Whether You Have a Place for It or Not

Buy it because you love it or because it's meaningful, especially art. Be willing to wait. Don't fill a room just because you feel like you have to. If there is a spot and you're waiting for the right table, put something there in the meantime, but be willing to wait. When you're traveling, think in terms of collecting art. The goal over time is for your home to reflect who you are and your life experiences, so it should be filled with people and places and events that are meaningful to you.

If you love it . . . get it. When you buy things you love, you'll find a place for them.

6. Use Things in Unexpected Ways

Using things in unexpected ways adds interest. I have an old drafting table I turned completely horizontal and I use it as an end table. You could use an old wooden toolbox as a centerpiece and put greenery in it. An old wagon wheel can be a pot rack. Remember a few years ago Restoration Hardware repurposed an old wheeled industrial cart as a coffee table? Yep, now they're showing up everywhere. And old pallets. Sarah Mae's husband, Jesse, is making gorgeous furniture from pallets—wooden platforms that likely held stacks of mulch for a couple of years at Home Depot. Be creative. Be willing to mix old and new. Juxtapose textures and time periods, but make sure that things feel complementary.

7. Don't Be Afraid to Get It Wrong

You don't get it right until you get it wrong a few times. You can always tweak and change things around. And when you're tired of something, move it to a different room in a different spot. It'll feel fresh just by giving it a new purpose.

8. Don't Buy Sets of Things

Buy individual pieces of furniture that you like. I'm not a huge fan of buying bedroom sets. Something sold in a set locks you in and there isn't much freedom to move items around. When you buy things that are all different, you can use them for multiple functions. If you get sick of a piece in one spot, move it somewhere else. If you have a bedroom set, you can't just remove an end table or you will have an odd piece. When you buy pieces you love, everything has an eclectic sort of feel, in addition to making it versatile.

9. Avoid Themed Spaces That Go Overboard

Let's say you love Winnie the Pooh. Maybe you can find a Pooh picture book at a resale shop, cut out some of the illustrations and frame them, use the color schemes from the book, or add a Pooh-ism quote on the wall, but don't buy Pooh bedding, window treatments, and wallpaper borders too. Be subtle. Think of creating threads of design more than themes.

10. Your Home Should Reflect Who You Are

So what if Pottery Barn says you should be into cream cable-knit throws and a gray sofa this fall? Maybe you're a colored-polka-dot-sofa kind of person. I mean, I know I am. So be the person you are! Your home should reflect YOU. Be you . . . because the worst thing ever is if you try to be someone else in your decorating and then end up feeling like a stranger in your own home. Blah! And no!

One final thing. Have fun with it. It's your space, so own it!

Four Handy Dandy Quick Tips to Help You in Your Cleaning Efforts

1. Get Your Kids to Help

For real! When my kiddos were babies, I was on my own. Granted, there was less mess, but there was still mess. And diapers. And exhaustion. But now, NOW, I have three little helpers and it is wonderful! I cannot stress enough the glory in having your children help. Besides the fact that it's good for them to learn how to work, it is actually a help.

Yes, you will have to train them and there might be some huffing and hawing, but eventually it will get better. I find that when we work together, things get done quickly and we are all happier. I'm always saying to my kids, "We are a team!" and the classic, "Many hands make light work!" I overhear my kids saying that phrase sometimes, and it makes me smile.

Keep on and your kids will be a delight and a help to you!

2. Accept That Good Enough Is Good Enough

I am a recovering perfectionist. My brand of perfectionism looked like this: "Oh, I can't get it all cleaned perfectly because I don't have time, so I just won't do it at all." Makes sense, right? NO! Of course it doesn't! It's better to do something than nothing!

And honestly, I'm learning that sometimes good enough *is* good enough. Maybe I didn't wash my windows, but I cleaned up my living room. Maybe I didn't dust the baseboards, but I swept up. Life just keeps on moving, and sometimes we have to be willing to let go of the details in order to keep on. It's okay.

When you have that magical day that affords you ALL THE TIME, go on and dust those baseboards. Or maybe you'll be able to hire someone to do that kind of detail work. But in the meantime, get what you need to get done and move on to enjoying your life!

3. Love Yourself

You are beautiful and glorious and colorful just the way you are! So what if you don't clean well and you're not detailed? You are made in the image of God, and you have the capacity to do great things for His Kingdom, which yes, oftentimes involves hidden things, like cleaning. But your identity should never be in what you do or don't do.

Love yourself because God wove you together and He loves you. You are not more holy because you clean well, and you are not less holy if you don't. Yes, cleaning is a part of life and it's a way to love others, but it has nothing to do with your identity. So crank the music up and dance yourself silly and get it done, but don't ever think for one second that you are a worse person or wife or mother because you don't rock at cleaning. Okay?

4. Slow It Down, Sister

Sometimes you've just got to put on a good podcast or some music and go slow—bit by bit.

Scrub the toilet slowly.

Take your time on the kitchen floor.

Go through your bookshelf, dusting and carefully placing your babies, I mean books, back on the shelf with love.

There can be a lovely rhythm to cleaning if we allow it. Sometimes the rush is good and fun and practical, but sometimes the *slow* is just what the soul needs.

Acknowledgments

MY DEEPEST THANKS TO:

Beth Buster—The genius who came up with the title of this book. Thank you so very much.

Christin Slade—My friend who came up with the idea for having Mary and Martha challenges. I know you don't remember coming up with this, but I do!

Bonne Steffen—The unsung hero in my books. Thank you once again for all your hard work!

Jen Ghionzoli—Utterly brilliant. Seriously, you are amazing and I want to keep you forever. Please design all my books forever—amen!

The whole Tyndale team—You all are just fantastic. It is an honor to work with you.

Sarah Zurin (my sister-in-law) and Susan Hoover (my mother-in-law)—Thank you for your contributions to this book! I am so grateful for you being in my life.

Logan Wolfram—Thank you for writing the foreword to this book and for being such a dear friend. I love you so.

Sally Clarkson—Thank you for teaching me what it means to have a hospitable, warm home filled with laughter and love. Your imprint on my soul will last forever.

Ella, Caedmon, and Caroline—Thank you for being the best kids in the whole world. You have made our home one of laughter and craziness and fun and dear memories. I love you so much.

Jesse—I love you. Thank you for your support and encouragement with each book. I would never have made it if it weren't for you.

And to all the readers who have supported this book since its infancy many years ago. You are the reason it is now in print after all this time!

Notes

KIND HOMEMAKING
1. See Micah 6:8.

WHAT DOES IT MEAN TO HAVE A MARTHA HOUSE THE MARY WAY?
1. Beth Buster is a mother of ten from Oklahoma whose blog site is *Anything but Ordinary*; http://bethbuster.blogspot.com/.
2. Christin Slade's blog and Daily Dose of God's Word can be found at http://www.christinslade.com/home/.

DAY 1: LIFTING LIFE ABOVE MERE EXISTENCE
1. Barbara K. Mouser, *Five Aspects of Woman: A Biblical Theology of Femininity* (Waxahachie, TX: International Council for Gender Studies, 2008), 3.9.

DAY 3: RHYTHM PRIORITIES
1. "The faithful love of the Lord never ends! . . . Great is his faithfulness; his mercies begin afresh each morning" (Lamentations 3:22-23, nlt).

DAY 6: OVERCOMING THE CURSE
1. Barbara K. Mouser, *Five Aspects of Woman: A Biblical Theology of Femininity* (Waxahachie, TX: International Council for Gender Studies, 2008), 1.15 (emphasis added).

DAY 9: TORNADO CLEANING
1. Professional organizer Marla Cilley (aka the FlyLady) suggests putting the timer on for fifteen minutes and going to work.

DAY 12: FEELING OVERWHELMED
1. Check out the FlyLady's website at flylady.net.
2. This was in response to a Facebook post, November 15, 2015.
3. Ibid.

DAY 13: PURGE, BABY, PURGE
1. Marie Kondo, *The Life-Changing Magic of Tidying Up* (Berkeley, CA: Ten Speed Press, 2014).
2. Ibid., 42.

DAY 15: KIDS AND CLEANING
1. Matthew 22:37-39
2. This was in response to a Facebook post, November 15, 2015.
3. Ibid.

DAY 16: I'D RATHER DO ANYTHING BUT CLEAN (WHEN THE BONES ARE FEELING LAZY)
1. See http://www.flylady.net/d/getting-started/flying-lessons/dressed-to-shoes.
2. Mark Twain is credited with the following quote: "If it's your job to eat a frog, it's best to do it first thing in the morning. And if it's your job to eat two frogs, it's best to eat the biggest one first." The phrase "Eat the frog" or "Eat that frog" has become another way of saying "Stop procrastinating."

DAY 19: FIGHTING FATIGUE
1. Colette Bouchez, "Top 10 Ways to Boost Your Energy," WebMD, http://www.webmd.com/women/features/10-energy-boosters.
2. Ibid.

DAY 20: DISTRACTIONS
1. I must confess that we've since resubscribed to Netflix as a way to unwind at the end of a long day. Sometimes a good binge is just what the soul needs.

DAY 23: TIME
1. Charles R. Swindoll, *Come Before Winter and Share My Hope* (Grand Rapids: Zondervan, 1994).

DAY 24: HELP! TO HIRE OR NOT TO HIRE
1. Blair Massey, "If I Only Had a Maid!" blog post on *Christian Homemaking*, July 31, 2009. Blair Massey is an organizational coach at http://www.keepingupathome.com.

DAY 25: THE THING WE ALL HAVE IN COMMON
1. See Harriet Braiker's website at http://www.harrietbraiker.com.

DAY 27: LAUNDRY BLUES
1. Renee Stam, http://www.babystam.blogspot.com/.
2. Kari Andres Kentner, http://goatfarmerswife.blogspot.com/.
3. This was in response to a Facebook post, no date available.
4. This was in response to a Facebook post, no date available.
5. Ingrid, http://www.reachinghiskids.blogspot.com/.
6. This was in response to a Facebook post, November 15, 2015.
7. Ibid.
8. Ibid.

DAY 28: WHO ARE YOU TRYING TO PLEASE?
1. This story first appeared in Sally Clarkson's book *Seasons of a Mother's Heart* (Monument, CO: Whole Heart Press, 2008), 60–62. Reprinted by permission of publisher. All rights reserved.

About the Author

SARAH MAE is a writer who encourages and inspires women to keep on and enjoy their lives right where they are. She is the author of *Longing for Paris: One Woman's Search for Joy, Beauty, and Adventure—Right Where She Is* and coauthor of *Desperate: Hope for the Mom Who Needs to Breathe* (with Sally Clarkson), and is a writer for the DaySpring blog, *(in) Courage*. She lives in Lancaster, Pennsylvania, with her husband and their three children, whom she homeschools. You can find her at SarahMae.com.

DISCOVER WHAT IT MEANS TO LIVE AN UNREGRETTABLE LIFE . . .

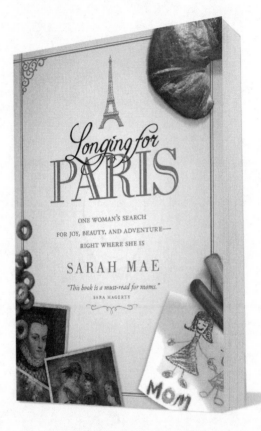

In *Longing for Paris*, Sarah Mae takes an honest look at the root of our deepest desires and shares her own story of bringing the light of Paris to her heart, marriage, and home. Join Sarah Mae in this delightful invitation to every woman who craves an abundant life, and find the joy of discovering your own adventure right where you are.

WWW.SARAHMAE.COM